MAP 1.

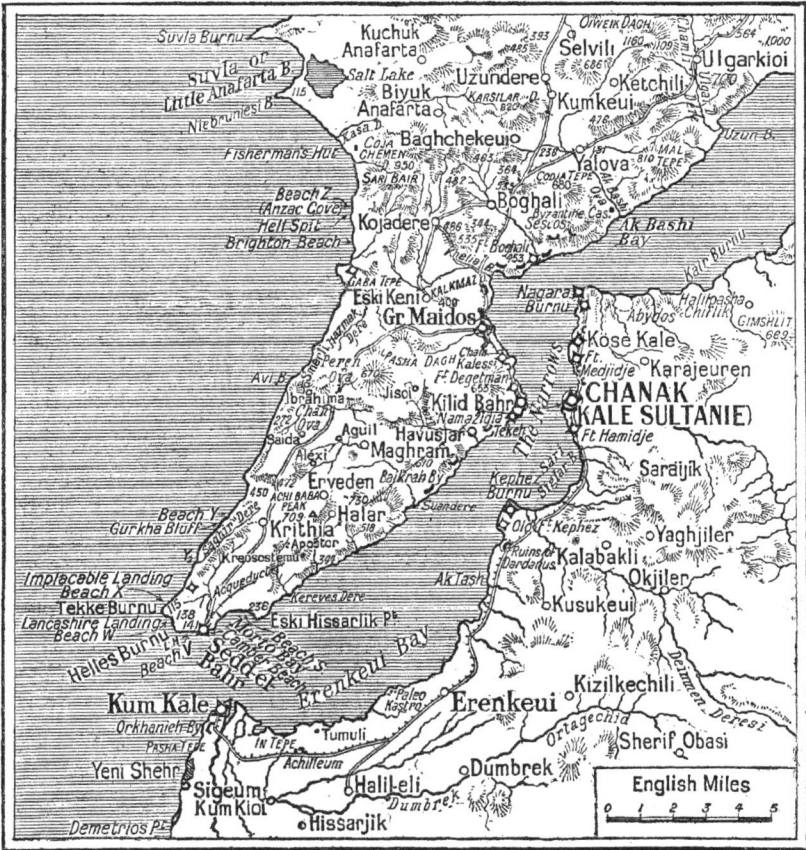

MAP OF THE GALLIPOLI PENINSULA
(By courtesy of the " Morning Post ")

www.ingramcontent.com/pod-product-compliance
Lightning Source LLC
Chambersburg PA
CBHW030932150426
42812CB00064B/2776/J

IAN HAMILTON'S
FINAL DESPATCH

WITH FIVE MAPS

LONDON
GEORGE NEWNES, LIMITED
1916

LIST OF MAPS

The following official notice is attached to the " London Gazette " containing the Final Despatch of Sir Ian Hamilton (which we have permission to reprint from the Controller of His Majesty's Stationery Office) —:

The issue of this despatch has been somewhat delayed for the preparation of an illustrative map ; but as this map cannot be completed until certain points have been investigated further, it has now been decided to issue the despatch without it. The map will be made available later.

WAR OFFICE, *January*, 1916.

IAN HAMILTON'S FINAL DESPATCH

War Office,
6th January, 1916.

The following despatch has been received by the Secretary of State for War from General Sir Ian Hamilton, G.C.B. : —

1, Hyde Park Gardens,
London, W.

11th December, 1915.

MY LORD,—

For the understanding of the operations about to be described I must first set forth the situation as it appeared to me early in July.

The three days' battle of the 6th–8th May had shown that neither of my forces, northern or southern, were strong enough to fight their way to the Narrows. On the 10th of May I had cabled asking that two fresh divisions might be sent me to enable me to press on and so prevent my attack degenerating into trench warfare. On the 17th of May I again cabled, saying that if we were going to be left to face Turkey on our own resources we should require two Army Corps additional to my existing forces at the Dardanelles.

The 52nd (Lowland) Division had been sent me, but between their dates of dispatch and arrival Russia had given up the idea of co-operating from the coast of the Black Sea. Thereby several Turkish divisions were set free for the Dardanelles, and the battle of the 4th June, locally successful as it was, found us just as weak, relatively, as we had been a month earlier.

During June Your Lordship became persuaded of the bearing of these facts, and I was promised three regular divisions plus the infantry of two Territorial divisions. The advance guard of these troops was due to reach Mudros by the 10th of July; by the 10th of August their concentration was to be complete.

THE ALTERNATIVES

Eliminating the impracticable, I had already narrowed down the methods of employing these fresh forces to one of the following four :—

(a) Every man to be thrown on to the southern sector of the Peninsula to force a way forward to the Narrows.

(b) Disembarkation on the Asiatic side of the Straits, followed by a march on Chanak.

(c) A landing at Enos or Ibrije for the purpose of seizing the neck of the isthmus at Bulair.

(d) Reinforcement of the Australian and New Zealand Army Corps, combined with a landing in Suvla Bay. Then with one strong push to capture Hill 305, and, working from that dominating point, to grip the waist of the Peninsula.

As to (a) I rejected that course—

(1) Because there were limits to the numbers which could be landed and deployed in one confined area.

(2) Because the capture of Krithia could no longer be counted upon to give us Achi Baba, an entirely new system of works having lately appeared upon the slopes of that mountain—works so planned that even if the enemy's western flank was turned and driven back from the coast the central and eastern portions of the mountain could still be maintained as a bastion to Kilid Bahr.

(3) Because if I tried to disengage myself both from Krithia and Achi Baba by landing due west of Kilid Bahr, my troops would be exposed to artillery fire from Achi Baba, the Olive Grove, and Kilid Bahr itself; the enemy's large reserves were too handy; there were not fair chances of success.

As to (b), although much of the Asiatic coast had now been wired and entrenched, the project was still attractive. Thereby the Turkish forces on the peninsula would be weakened; our beaches at Cape Helles would be freed from Asiatic shells; the threat to the enemy's sea communications was obvious.

But when I descended into detail I found that the expected reinforcements would not run to a double operation.   I mean that, unless I could make a thorough, whole-hearted attack on the enemy in the peninsula, I should reap no advantage in that theatre from the transference of the Turkish peninsula troops to reinforce Asia, whereas, if the British forces landed in Asia were not strong enough in themselves seriously to threaten Chanak, the Turks for their part would not seriously relax their grip upon the peninsula.

NAVAL OBJECTIONS

To cut the land communications of the whole of the Turkish peninsular army, as in (c), was a better scheme on paper than on the spot.   The naval objections appeared to my coadjutor, Vice-Admiral de Robeck, well-nigh insurmountable.   Already, owing to submarine dangers, all reinforcements, ammunition, and supplies had to be brought up from Mudros to Helles or Anzac by night in fleet-sweepers and trawlers.   A new landing near Bulair would have added another 50 miles to the course such small craft must cover, thus placing too severe a strain upon the capacities of the flotilla.

The landing promised special hazards owing to the difficulty of securing the transports and covering ships from submarine attack.   Ibrije has a bad beach, and the distance to Enos, the only point suitable to a disembarkation on a large scale, was so great that the enemy would have had time to organise a formidable opposition from his garrisons in Thrace. Four divisions at least would be required to overcome such opposition. These might now be found; but, even so, and presupposing every other obstacle overcome, it was by no manner of means certain that the Turkish army on the peninsula would thereby be brought to sue for terms, or that the Narrows would thereby be opened to the Fleet. The enemy would still be able to work supplies across the Straits from Chanak.

The swiftness of the current, the shallow draft of the Turkish lighters, the guns of the forts, made it too difficult even for our dauntless submarine commanders to paralyse movement across these land-locked waters. To achieve that purpose I must bring my artillery fire to bear both on the land and water communications of the enemy.

STORMING HILL 305

This brings me to (d), the storming of that dominating height, Hill 305, with the capture of Maidos and Gaba Tepe as its sequel.

From the very first I had hoped that by landing a force under the heights of Sari Bair we should be able to strangle the Turkish communications to the southwards, whether by land or sea, and so clear the Narrows for the Fleet. Owing to the enemy's superiority, both in numbers and in position; owing to under-estimates of the strength of the original entrenchments prepared and sited under German direction; owing to the constant dwindling of the units of my force through wastage; owing also to the intricacy and difficulty of the terrain, these hopes had not hitherto borne fruit. But they were well founded. So much at least had clearly enough been demonstrated by the desperate and costly nature of the Turkish attacks. The Australians and New Zealanders had rooted themselves in very near to the vitals of the enemy. By their tenacity and courage they still held open the doorway from which one strong thrust forward might give us command of the Narrows.

From the naval point of view the auspices were also favourable. Suvla Bay was but one mile further from Mudros than Anzac, and its possession would ensure us a submarine-proof base and a harbour good against gales, excepting those from the south-west. There were, as might be expected, some special difficulties to be overcome. The broken, intricate country—the lack of water—the consequent anxious supply questions. Of these it can only be said that a bad country is better than an entrenched country, and that supply and water problems may be countered by careful preparation.

Before a man of the reinforcements had arrived my mind was made up as to their employment, and by means of a vigorous offensive from Anzac, combined with a surprise landing to the north of it, I meant to try and win through to Maidos, leaving behind me a well-protected line of communications starting from the bay of Suvla.

THE DANGERS OF DELAY

Another point which had to be fixed in advance was the date. The new troops would gain in fighting value if they could first be given a turn in the trenches. So much was clear. But the relief of the troops already holding those trenches would have been a long and difficult task for the Navy, and time was everything, seeing that everywhere the enemy was digging in as fast as he possibly could dig. Also, where large numbers of troops were to be smuggled into Anzac and another large force was to land by surprise at Suvla, it was essential to eliminate the moon. Unless the plunge could be taken by the second week in August the whole venture must be postponed for a month. The dangers of such delay were clear. To realise them I had only to consider how notably my prospects would have been bettered had these same reinforcements arrived in time to enable me to anticipate the moon of July.

Place and date having shaped themselves, the intervening period had to be filled in with as much fighting as possible. First, to gain ground; secondly, to maintain the moral ascendancy which my troops had by this time established; thirdly, to keep the enemy's eyes fixed rather upon Helles than Anzac.

Working out my ammunition allowance, I found

I could accumulate just enough high explosive shell to enable me to deliver one serious attack per each period of three weeks. I was thus limited to a single effort on the large scale, plus a prescribed unceasing offensive routine, with bombing, sniping, and mining as its methods.

TURKISH RIGHT DRIVEN BACK.

The action of the 12th and 13th of July was meant to be a sequel to the action of the 28th June. That advance had driven back the Turkish right on to their second main system of defence just south of Krithia. But, on my centre and right, the enemy still held their forward system of trenches, and it was my intention on the 12th July to seize the remaining trenches of this foremost system from the sea at the mouth of the Kereves Dere to the main Sedd-el-Bahr—Krithia road, along a front of some 2,000 yards.

On our right the attack was to be entrusted to the French Corps; on the right centre to the 52nd (Lowland) Division. On the 52nd Division's front the operation was planned to take place in two phases : our right was to attack in the morning, our left in the afternoon. Diversions by the 29th Division on the left of the southern section and at Anzac were to take place on the same day, so as to prevent the enemy's reserves from reinforcing the real point of attack.

Scottish Borderers' Tragedy

At 7.35 a.m., after a heavy bombardment, the troops, French and Scottish, dashed out of their trenches and at once captured two lines of enemy trenches. Pushing forward with fine *élan,* the 1st Division of the French Corps completed the task assigned to it by carrying the whole of the Turkish forward system of works, namely, the line of trenches skirting the lower part of the Kereves Dere. Further to the left the 2nd French Division and our 155th Brigade maintained the two lines of trenches they had gained. But on the left of the 155th Brigade the 4th Battalion, King's Own Scottish Borderers, pressed on too eagerly. They not only carried the third line of trenches, but charged on up the hill and beyond the third line, then advanced indeed until they came under the *feu de barrage* of the French artillery. Nothing could live under so cruel a cross-fire from friend and foe, so the King's Own Scottish Borderers were forced to fall back with heavy losses to the second line of enemy trenches which they had captured in their first rush.

During this fighting telephone wires from forward positions were cut by enemy's shell fire, and here and there in the elaborate network of trenches numbers of Turks were desperately resisting to the last. Thus though the second line of captured trenches continued to be held as a whole, much confused fighting ensued; there were retirements

B

in parts of the line, reserves were rapidly being used up, and generally the situation was anxious and uncertain. But the best way of clearing it up seemed to be to deliver the second phase of the attack by the 157th Brigade just as it had originally been arranged. Accordingly, after a preliminary bombardment, the 157th Brigade rushed forward under heavy machine-gun and rifle fire, and splendidly carried the whole of the enemy trenches allotted as their objective. Here, then, our line had advanced some 400 yards, while the 155th Brigade and the 2nd French Division had advanced between 200 and 300 yards. At 6 p.m. the 52nd Division was ordered to make the line good; it seemed to be fairly in our grasp.

All night long determined counter-attacks, one after another, were repulsed by the French and the 155th Brigade, but about 7.30 a.m. the right of the 157th Brigade gave way before a party of bombers, and our grip upon the enemy began to weaken.

Errors of Impetuosity

I therefore decided that three battalions of the Royal Naval Division should reinforce a fresh attack to be made that afternoon, 13th July, on such portions of our original objectives as remained in the enemy's hands. This second attack was a success. The 1st French Division pushed their right down to the mouth of the Kereves Dere; the 2nd French Division attacked the trenches they had failed to take on the preceding day; the Nelson Battalion, on the left of the Royal Naval Division attack, valiantly advanced and made good, well supported by the artillery of the French. The Portsmouth Battalion, pressing on too far, fell into precisely the same error at precisely the same spot as did the 4th King's Own Scottish Borderers on the 12th, an over-impetuosity which cost them heavy losses.

The 1/5th Royal Scots Fusiliers, commanded by Lieutenant-Colonel J. B. Pollok-McCall; the 1/7th Royal Scots, commanded by Lieutenant-Colonel W. C. Peebles; the 1/5th King's Own Scottish Borderers, commanded by Lieutenant-Colonel W. J. Millar; and the 1/6th Highland Light Infantry, commanded by Major J. Anderson, are mentioned as having specially distinguished themselves in this engagement.

Generally, the upshot of the attack was this. On our right and on the French left two lines had been captured, but in neither case was the third, or last, line of the system in their hands. Elsewhere a fine feat of arms had been accomplished, and a solid and enduring advance had been achieved, giving us far the best sited line for defence with much the best field for machine-gun and rifle fire we had hitherto obtained upon the peninsula.

PRISONERS AND CASUALTIES

A machine-gun and 200 prisoners were captured by the French; the British took a machine-gun and 329 prisoners. The casualties in the French Corps were not heavy, though it is with sorrow that I have to report the mortal wound of General Masnou, commanding the 1st Division. Our own casualties were a little over 3,000; those of the enemy about 5,000.

On 17th Jüly Lieutenant-General Hunter Weston, commanding the 8th Corps, left the peninsula for a few days' rest, and, to my very deep regret, was subsequently invalided home. I have already drawn attention to his invincible self-confidence, untiring energy, and trained ability.

As I was anxious to give the Commander of the new troops all the local experience possible, I appointed Lieutenant-General Hon. Sir Frederick Stopford, whose own Corps were now assembling at Mudros, temporarily to succeed Lieutenant-General Hunter Weston, but on 24th July, when General Stopford had to set to work with his own Corps, Major-General W. Douglas, General Officer Commanding 42nd Division, took over temporary command of the 8th Corps; while Major-General W. R. Marshall, General Officer Commanding 87th Brigade, assumed temporary command of the 42nd Division.

"Tasmania Post" Threatened

Only one other action need be mentioned before coming to the big operations of August. On the extreme right of Anzac the flank of a work called Tasmania Post was threatened by the extension of a Turkish trench. The task of capturing this trench was entrusted to the 3rd Australian Brigade. After an artillery bombardment, mines were to be fired, whereupon four columns of 50 men each were to assault and occupy specified lengths of the trench. The regiment supplying the assaulting columns was the 11th Australian Infantry Battalion.

At 10.15 p.m. on 31st July the bombardment was opened. Ten minutes later and the mines were duly fired. The four assaulting parties dashed forward at once, crossed our own barbed wire on planks, and were into the craters before the whole of the *débris* had fallen. Total casualties: 11 killed and 74 wounded; Turkish killed, 100.

Arrival of Reinforcements

By the time this action was fought a large proportion of my reinforcements had arrived, and, on the same principle which induced me to put General Stopford in temporary command at Helles, I relieved the war-worn 29th Division at the same place by the 13th Division under Major-General Shaw. The experiences here gained, in looking after themselves, in forgetting the thousand and one details of peace soldiering and in grasping the two or three elementary rules of conduct in war soldiering, were, it turned out, to be of priceless advantage to the 13th Division throughout the heavy fighting of the following month.

TIME AND MOON

And now it was time to determine a date for the great venture. The moon would rise on the morning of the 7th at about 2 o'clock. A day or two previously the last reinforcements, the 53rd and 54th Divisions, were due to arrive. The first day of the attack was fixed for the 6th of August.

Once the date was decided a certain amount of ingenuity had to be called into play so as to divert the attention of the enemy from my main strategical conception. This—I repeat for the sake of clearness—was :—

(1) To break out with a rush from Anzac and cut off the bulk of the Turkish Army from land communication with Constantinople.

(2) To gain such a command for my artillery as to cut off the bulk of the Turkish Army from sea traffic whether with Constantinople or with Asia.

(3) Incidentally, to secure Suvla Bay as a winter base for Anzac and all the troops operating in the northern theatre.

A SURPRISE LANDING

My schemes for hoodwinking the Turks fell under two heads : First, strategical diversions, meant to draw away enemy reserves not yet committed to the peninsula. Secondly, tactical diversions meant to hold up enemy reserves already on the peninsula. Under the first heading came a surprise landing by a force of 300 men on the northern shore of the Gulf of Xeros ; demonstrations by French ships opposite Mitylene along the Syrian coast ; concentration at Mitylene ; inspections at Mitylene by the Admiral and myself ; making to order of a whole set of maps of Asia in Egypt, as well as secret service work, most of which bore fruit.

Amongst the tactical diversions were a big containing attack at Helles ; soundings, registration of guns, &c., by monitors between Gaba Tepe and Kum Tepe ; an attack to be carried out by Anzac on Lone Pine trenches, which lay in front of their right wing and as far distant as the local terrain would admit from the scene of the real battle. Thanks entirely to the reality and vigour which the Navy and the troops threw into them, each one of these ruses was, it so turned out, entirely successful, with the result that the Turks, despite their excellent spy system, were caught completely off their guard at dawn on the 7th of August.

STAFF DIFFICULTIES

Having settled upon the manner and time of the diversions, orders had to be issued for the main operation. And here I must pause a moment to draw your Lordship's attention to the extraordinary complexity of the staff work caused by the unique distribution of my forces. Within the narrow confines of the positions I held on the peninsula it was impossible to concentrate even as much as one-third of the fresh troops about to be launched to the attack. Nor could Mudros and Imbros combined absorb the whole of the remainder. The strategic concentration which precedes a normal battle had in my case to be a very wide dispersion. Thus of the forces destined for my offensive, on the day before the battle, part were at Anzac, part at Imbros, part at Mudros, and part at Mitylene. These last three detachments were separated respectively by 14, 60, and 120 miles of sea from the arena into which they were simultaneously to appear.

To ensure the punctual arrival of all these masses of inexperienced troops at the right moment and spot, together with their material, munitions, stores, supplies, water, animals, and vehicles, was a prodigious undertaking demanding not only

competence, but self-confidence; and I will say
for my General Staff that I believe the clearness and completeness of their orders for this
concentration and landing will hereafter be studied
as models in military academies. The need for
economy in sea transport, the awkwardness and
restriction of open beaches, the impossibility of
landing guns, animals, or vehicles rapidly—all
these made it essential to create a special, separate
organisation for every single unit taking part in
the adventure. A pack mule corps to supply
80,000 men had also to be organised for that specific
purpose until such time as other transport could
be landed.

A 30,000-GALLON RESERVOIR

As to water, that element of itself was responsible for a whole chapter of preparations. An
enormous quantity had to be collected secretly,
and as secretly stowed away at Anzac, where a
high-level reservoir had to be built, having a
holding capacity of 30,000 gallons, and fitted out
with a regular system of pipes and distribution
tanks. A stationary engine was brought over
from Egypt to fill that reservoir. Petroleum tins,
with a carrying capacity of 80,000 gallons, were
got together, and fixed up with handles, &c., but
the collision of the *Moorgate* with another vessel
delayed the arrival of large numbers of these just as
a breakdown in the stationary engine upset for a

while the well-laid plan of the high-level reservoir. But Anzac was ever resourceful in face of misadventures, and when the inevitable accidents arose it was not with folded hands that they were met.

Turning to Suvla Bay, it was believed that good wells and springs existed both in the Biyuk, Anafarta Valley, and in Suvla Bay. But nothing so vital could possibly be left to hearsay, and although, as it turned out, our information was perfectly correct, yet the War Office were asked to dispatch with each reinforcing division water receptacles for pack transport at the rate of half a gallon per man.

PRAISE FOR THE NAVY

The sheet-anchor on which hung the whole of these elaborate schemes was the Navy. One tiny flaw in the perfect mutual trust and confidence animating the two Services would have wrecked the whole enterprise. Experts at a distance may have guessed as much; it was self-evident to the rawest private on the spot. But with men like Vice-Admiral de Robeck, Commodore Roger Keyes, Rear-Admiral Christian, and Captain F. H. Mitchell at our backs, we soldiers were secured against any such risk, and it will be seen how perfect was the precision the sailors put into their job.

The hour was now approaching, and I waited

for it with as much confidence as is possible when to the inevitable uncertainties of war are to be added those of the weather. Apart from feints, the first blow was to be dealt in the southern zone.

COMMUNICATION DIFFICULTIES

In that theatre I had my own Poste de Commandement. But upon the 6th of August attacks in the south were only to form a subsidiary part of one great concerted attack. Anzac was to deliver the knock-down blow; Helles and Suvla were complementary operations. Were I to commit myself at the outset to any one of these three theatres I must lose my sense of proportion. Worse, there being no lateral communication between them, as soon as I landed at one I was cut off from present touch with both of the others. At Imbros I was 45 minutes from Helles, 40 minutes from Anzac, and 50 minutes from Suvla. Imbros was the centre of the cable system, and thence I could follow each phase of the triple attack and be ready with my two divisions of reserve to throw in reinforcements where they seemed most to be required. Therefore I decided to follow the opening moves from General Headquarters.

At Helles the attack of the 6th was directed against 1,200 yards of the Turkish front opposite our own right and right centre, and was to be carried out by the 88th Brigade of the 29th Division. Two small Turkish trenches enfilading the main advance had, if possible, to be captured simultaneously, an affair which was entrusted to the 42nd Division.

ENEMY'S OBSTINATE DEFENCE

After bombardment the infantry assaulted at 3.50 p.m. On the left large sections of the enemy's line were carried, but on our centre and right the Turks were encountered in masses, and the attack, pluckily and perseveringly as it was pressed, never had any real success. The 1st Battalion, Essex Regiment, in particular forced their way into the crowded enemy trench opposite them, despite the most determined resistance, but, once in, were subjected to the heaviest musketry fire from both flanks, as well as in reverse, and were shattered by showers of bombs. Two separate resolute attacks were made by the 42nd Division, but both of them recoiled in face of the unexpected volume of fire developed by the Turks.

After dark officer's patrols were sent up to ascertain the exact position of affairs. Heavy Turkish counter-attacks were being pressed against such portions of the line we still retained. Many of our men fought it out where they stood to the last, but by nightfall none of the enemy's line remained in our possession.

Our set-back was in no wise the fault of the troops. That ardour which only dashed itself to pieces against the enemy's strong entrenchments and numerous, stubborn defenders on the 6th of August would, a month earlier, have achieved notable success. Such was the opinion of all.

MAP 2.

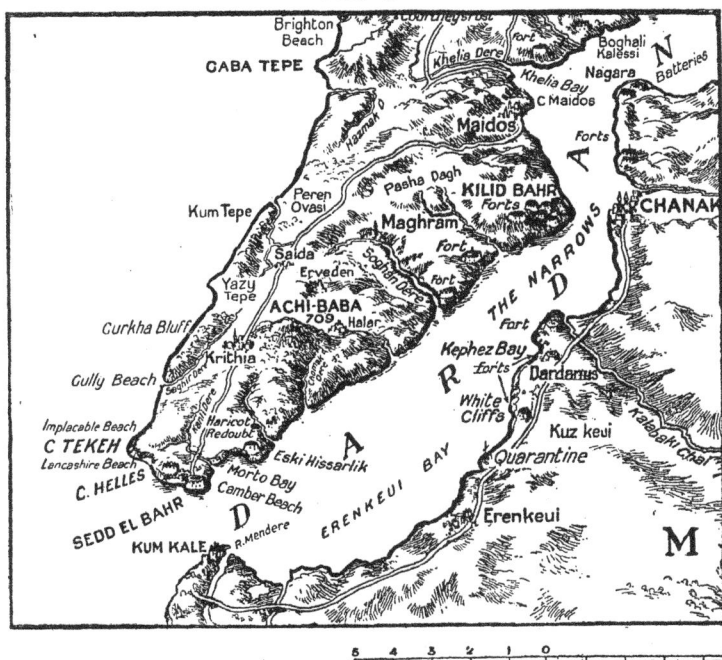

But the *moral* as well as the strength of the Turks had had time to rise to great heights since our last serious encounters with them on the 21st and 28th of June and on the 12th of July. On those dates all ranks had felt, as an army feels, instinctively, yet with certitude, that they had fairly got the upper hand of the enemy, and that, given the wherewithal, they could have gone on steadily advancing. Now that selfsame, half-beaten enemy were again making as stout a resistance as they had offered us at our original landing !

Turks Advertise by Posters

For this recovery of the Turks there were three reasons : one moral, one material, and one fortuitous.

(1) The news of the enemy's advance on the Eastern front had come to hand and had been advertised to us on posters from the Turkish trenches before we heard about it from home.

(2) Two new divisions had come down south to Helles to replace those we had most severely handled.

(3) The enemy trenches selected for our attack were found to be packed with troops and so were their communication trenches, the reason being, as explained to us by prisoners, that the Turkish Commander had meant to launch from them an attack upon us. We had, in fact, by a coincidence as strange as it was unlucky, anticipated a Turkish offensive by an hour or two at most !

Sure enough, next morning, the enemy in their turn attacked the left of the line from which our own troops had advanced to the assault. A few of them gained a footing in our trenches and were all killed or captured. The remainder were driven back by fire.

COMMANDER-IN-CHIEF'S OBJECTIVE

As the aim of my action in this southern zone was to advance if I could, but in any case to contain the enemy and prevent him reinforcing to the northwards, I persevered on the 7th with my plans, notwithstanding the counter-attack of the Turks which was actually in progress. My objective this time was a double line of Turkish trenches on a front of about 800 yards between the Mal Tepe Dere and the west branch of the Kanli Dere. After a preliminary bombardment the troops of the 125th Brigade on the right and the 129th on the left made the assault at 9.40 a.m. From the outset it was evident that the enemy were full of fight and in great force, and that success would only be gained after a severe struggle.

On the right and on the centre the first enemy line was captured, and small parties pushed on to the second line, where they were unable to maintain themselves for long. On the left but little ground was gained, and by 11 a.m. what little had been taken had been relinquished. But in the centre a stiff battle raged all day up and down a vineyard some 200 yards long by 100 yards broad on the west of the Krithia road. A large portion of the vineyard had been captured in the first dash, and the East Lancashire men in this part of the field gallantly stood their ground here against a succession of vigorous counter-attacks.

The enemy suffered very severely in these counter-attacks, which were launched in strength and at short intervals. Both our Brigades had also lost heavily during the advance and in repelling the fierce onslaughts of the enemy, but, owing to the fine endurance of the 6th and 7th Battalions of the Lancashire Fusiliers, it was found possible to hold the vineyard through the night, and a massive column of the enemy which strove to overwhelm their thinned ranks was shattered to pieces in the attempt.

The Grit of the Lancastrians

On 8th August Lieutenant-General Sir F. J. Davies took over command of the 8th Army Corps, and Major-General W. Douglas reverted to the command of the 42nd Division. For two more days his troops were called upon to show their qualities of vigilance and power of determined resistance, for the enemy had by no means yet lost hope of wresting from us the ground we had won in the vineyard. This unceasing struggle was a supreme test for battalions already exhausted by 48 hours' desperate fighting and weakened by the loss of so many good leaders and men; but the peculiar grit of the Lancastrians was equal to the strain, and they did not fail.

Two specially furious counter-attacks were delivered by the Turks on the 8th August, one at 4.40 a.m., the other at 8.30 p.m., where again our bayonets were too much for them. Throughout the night they made continuous bomb attacks, but the 6th Lancashire Fusiliers and the 4th East Lancashire Regiment stuck gamely to their task at the eastern corner of the vineyard. There was desperate fighting also at the northern corner, where the personal bravery of Lieutenant W. T. Forshaw, 1/9th Manchester Regiment, who stuck to his post after his detachment had been relieved (an act for which he has since been awarded the V.C.), was largely instrumental in the repulse of three very determined onslaughts.

THE BOMBERS' VICTORY

By the morning of the 9th August things were quieter, and the sorely tried troops were relieved. On the night of the 12th/13th the enemy made one more sudden, desperate dash for their vineyard —and got it! But, on the 13th, our bombers took the matter in hand. The Turks were finally driven out; the new fire trenches were wired and loopholed, and have since become part of our line.

These two attacks had served their main pur-

C

pose. If the local successes were not all that had been hoped for, yet a useful advance had been achieved, and not only had they given a fresh, hard fighting enemy more than he had bargained for, but they had actually drawn down Turkish reinforcements to their area. And how can a Commander say enough for the troops who, aware that their task was only a subsidiary one, fought with just as much vim and resolution as if they were storming the battlements of Constantinople.

GENERAL BIRDWOOD'S FORCES

I will now proceed to tell of the assault on Chunuk Bair by the forces under General Birdwood, and of the landing of the 9th Corps in the neighbourhood of Suvla Bay. The entire details of the operations allotted to the troops to be employed in the Anzac area were formulated by Lieutenant-General Birdwood, subject only to my final approval.

So excellently was this vital business worked out on the lines of the instructions issued that I had no modifications to suggest, and all these local preparations were completed by 6th August in a way which reflects the greatest credit not only on the Corps Commander and his staff, but also upon the troops themselves, who had to toil like slaves to accumulate food, drink, and munitions of war. Alone the accommodation for the extra troops to be landed necessitated an immense amount of work in preparing new concealed bivouacs, in making interior communications, and in storing water and supplies, for I was determined to put on shore as many fighting men as our modest holding at Anzac could possibly accommodate or provision.

All the work was done by Australian and New Zealand soldiers almost entirely by night, and the uncomplaining efforts of these much-tried troops in preparation are in a sense as much to their credit as their heroism in the battles that followed.

THE WATER PROBLEM AGAIN

Above all, the water problem caused anxiety to the Admiral, to Lieutenant-General Birdwood, and to myself. The troops to advance from Suvla Bay across the Anafarta valley might reckon on finding some wells—it was certain, at least, that no water was waiting for us on the crests of the ridges of Sari Bair! Therefore, first, several days' supply had to be stocked into tanks along the beach and thence pumped up into other tanks halfway up the mountains; secondly, a system of mule transport had to be worked out so that, in so far as was humanly possible thirst should not be allowed to overcome the troops after they had overcome the difficulties of the country and the resistance of the enemy.

C 2

REINFORCEMENTS BY NIGHT

On the nights of the 4th, 5th, and 6th August the reinforcing troops were shipped into Anzac very silently at the darkest hours. Then, still silently, they were tucked away from enemy aeroplanes or observatories in their prepared hiding-places. The whole sea route lay open to the view of the Turks upon Achi Baba's summit and Battleship Hill. Aeroplanes could count every tent and every ship at Mudros or at Imbros. Within rifle fire of Anzac's open beach hostile riflemen were looking out across the Ægean no more than twenty feet from our opposing lines.

Every modern appliance of telescope, telegraph, wireless was at the disposal of the enemy. Yet the instructions worked out at General Headquarters in the minutest detail (the result of conferences with the Royal Navy, which were attended by Brigadier-General Skeen, of General Birdwood's Staff) were such that the scheme was carried through without a hitch. The preparation of the ambush was treated as a simple matter by the services therein engaged, and yet I much doubt whether any more pregnant enterprise than this of landing so large a force under the very eyes of the enemy, and of keeping them concealed there three days, is recorded in the annals of war.

Divisions and Brigades.

The troops now at the disposal of General Birdwood amounted in round numbers to 37,000 rifles and 72 guns, with naval support from two cruisers, four monitors, and two destroyers. Under the scheme these troops were to be divided into two main portions. The task of holding the existing Anzac position, and of making frontal assaults therefrom, was assigned to the Australian Division (plus the 1st and 3rd Light Horse Brigades and two battalions of the 40th Brigade); that of assaulting the Chunuk Bair ridge was entrusted to the New Zealand and Australian Division (less the 1st and 3rd Light Horse Brigades), to the 13th Division (less five battalions), and to the 29th Indian Infantry Brigade and to the Indian Mounted Artillery Brigade. The 29th Brigade of the 10th Division (less one battalion) and the 38th Brigade were held in reserve.

The Assault on Lone Pine

The most simple method of developing this complicated series of operations will be first to take the frontal attacks from the existing Anzac position, and afterwards to go on to the assault on the more distant ridges. During the 4th, 5th, and 6th of August the works on the enemy's left and centre were subjected to a slow bombardment, and on the afternoon of the 6th August an assault was made upon the formidable Lone Pine entrenchment. Although, in its essence, a diversion to draw the enemy's attention and reserves from the grand attack impending upon his right, yet, in itself, Lone Pine was a distinct step on the way across to Maidos. It commanded one of the main sources of the Turkish water supply, and was a work, or, rather, a series of works, for the safety of which the enemy had always evinced a certain nervousness. The attack was designed to heighten this impression.

WIRE ENTANGLEMENTS

The work consisted of a strong *point d'appui* on the south-western end of a plateau, where it confronted, at distances varying from 60 to 120 yards, the salient in the line of our trenches named by us the Pimple. The entrenchment was evidently very strong; it was entangled with wire, and provided with overhead cover, and it was connected by numerous communication trenches with another *point d'appui* known as Johnston's Jolly on the north, as well as with two other works on the east and south. The frontage for attack amounted at most to some 220 yards, and the approaches lay open to heavy enfilade fire, both from the north and from the south.

The detailed scheme of attack was worked out with care and forethought by Major-General H. B. Walker, commanding 1st Australian Division, and his thoroughness contributed, I consider, largely to the success of the enterprise.

The action commenced at 4.30 p.m. with a continuous and heavy bombardment of the Lone Pine and adjacent trenches, H.M.S. *Bacchante* assisting by searching the valleys to the north-east and east, and the monitors by shelling the enemy's batteries south of Gaba Tepe.

"A RACE AGAINST DEATH"

The assault had been entrusted to the 1st Australian Brigade (Brigadier-General N. M. Smyth), and punctually at 5.30 p.m. it was carried out by the 2nd, 3rd, and 4th Australian Battalions, the 1st Battalion forming the Brigade reserve. Two lines left their trenches simultaneously, and were closely followed up by a third. The rush across the open was a regular race against death, which came in the shape of a hail of shell and rifle bullets from front and from either flank. But the Australians had firmly resolved to reach the enemy's trenches, and in this determination they became for the moment invincible.

The barbed-wire entanglement was reached and was surmounted.

Then came a terrible moment, when it seemed as though it would be physically impossible to penetrate into the trenches. The overhead cover of stout pine beams resisted all individual efforts to move it, and the loopholes continued to spit fire. Groups of our men then bodily lifted up the beams and individual soldiers leaped down into the semi-darkened galleries amongst the Turks. By 5.47 p.m. the 3rd and 4th Battalions were well into the enemy's vitals, and a few minutes later the reserves of the 2nd Battalion advanced over their parados, and driving out, killing, or capturing the occupants, made good the whole of the trenches. The reserve companies of the 3rd and 4th Battalions followed, and at 6.20 p.m. the 1st Battalion (in reserve) was launched to consolidate the position.

VIOLENT COUNTER-ATTACKS

At once the Turks made it plain, as they have never ceased to do since, that they had no intention of acquiescing in the capture of this capital work. At 7.0 p.m. a determined and violent counter-attack began, both from the north and from the south. Wave upon wave the enemy swept forward with the bayonet. Here and there a well-directed salvo of bombs emptied a section of a trench, but whenever this occurred the gap was quickly filled by the initiative of the officers and the gallantry of the men.

The enemy allowed small respite. At 1.30 that night the battle broke out afresh. Strong parties of Turks swarmed out of the communication trenches, preceded by showers of bombs. For seven hours these counter-attacks continued. All this time consolidation was being attempted, although the presence of so many Turkish prisoners hampered movement and constituted an actual danger. In beating off these desperate counter-attacks very heavy casualties were suffered by the Australians. Part of the 12th Battalion, the reserve of the 3rd Brigade, had therefore to be thrown into the *mêlée*.

Enemy's Sustained Efforts

Twelve hours later, at 1.30 p.m. on the 7th, another effort was made by the enemy, lasting uninterruptedly at closest quarters till 5 p.m., then being resumed at midnight and proceeding intermittently till dawn. At an early period of this last counter-attack the 4th Battalion were forced by bombs to relinquish portion of a trench, but later on, led by their commanding officer, Lieutenant-Colonel McNaghten, they killed every Turk who had got in.

During the 8th of August advantage was taken of every cessation in the enemy's bombing to consolidate. The 2nd Battalion, which had lost its commanding officer and suffered especially severely, was withdrawn and replaced by the 7th Battalion, the reserve to the 2nd Infantry Brigade.

TURKS DEMORALISED

At 5 a.m. on 9th August the enemy made a sudden attempt to storm from the east and south-east after a feint of fire attack from the north. The 7th Battalion bore the brunt of the shock, and handled the attack so vigorously that by 7.45 a.m. there were clear signs of demoralisation in the enemy's ranks. But, although this marked the end of counter-attacks on the large scale, the bombing and sniping continued, though in less volume, throughout this day and night, and lasted till 12th August, when it at last became manifest that we had gained complete ascendancy.

During the final grand assault our losses from artillery fire were large, and ever since the work has passed into our hands it has been a favourite daily and nightly mark for heavy shells and bombs.

THE IRRESISTIBLE AUSTRALIANS

Thus was Lone Pine taken and held. The Turks were in great force and very full of fight, yet one weak Australian brigade, numbering at the outset but 2,000 rifles, and supported only by two weak battalions, carried the work under the eyes of a whole enemy division, and maintained their grip upon it like a vice during six days' successive counter-attacks. High praise is due to Brigadier-General N. M. Smyth and to his battalion commanders. The irresistible dash and daring of officers and men in the initial charge were a glory to Australia. The stout-heartedness with which they clung to the captured ground in spite of fatigue, severe losses, and the continual strain of shell fire and bomb attacks may seem less striking to the civilian; it is even more admirable to the soldier.

From start to finish the artillery support was untiring and vigilant. Owing to the rapid, accurate fire of the 2nd New Zealand Battery, under Major Sykes, several of the Turkish onslaughts were altogether defeated in their attempts to get to grips with the Australians. Not a chance was lost by these gunners, although time and again the enemy's artillery made direct hits on their shields. The hand-to-hand fighting in the semi-obscurity of the trenches was prolonged and very bitterly contested. In one corner eight Turks and six Australians were found lying as they had bayoneted one another. To make room for the fighting men the dead were ranged in rows on either side of the gangway. After the first violence of the counter-attacks had abated, 1,000 corpses—our own and Turkish—were dragged out from the trenches.

HEAVY CASUALTIES

For the severity of our own casualties some partial consolation may be found in the facts, first, that those of the enemy were much heavier, our guns and machine-guns having taken toll of them as they advanced in mass formation along the reverse slopes; secondly, that the Lone Pine attack drew all the local enemy reserves towards it, and may be held, more than any other cause, to have been the reason that the Suvla Bay landing was so lightly opposed, and that comparatively few of the enemy were available at first to reinforce against our attack on Sari Bair. Our captures in this feat of arms amounted to 134 prisoners, seven machine-guns, and a large quantity of ammunition and equipment.

Other frontal attacks from the existing Anzac positions were not so fortunate. They fulfilled their object in so far as they prevented the enemy from reinforcing against the attack upon the high ridges, but they failed to make good any ground. Taken in sequence of time, they included an attack upon the work known as German Officers' Trench, on the extreme right of our line, at midnight on August 6th/7th, also assaults on the Nek and Baby 700 trenches opposite the centre of our line, delivered at 4.30 a.m. on the 7th. The 2nd Australian Brigade did all that men could do; the 8th Light Horse only accepted their repulse after losing

three-fourths of that devoted band who so bravely
sallied forth from Russell's Top.

CONCEALED MACHINE-GUNS

Some of the works were carried, but in these
cases the enemy's concealed machine-guns made
it impossible to hold on.   But all that day, as the
result of these most gallant attacks, Turkish reserves
on Battleship Hill were being held back to meet
any dangerous development along the front of the
old Anzac line, and so were not available to meet
our main enterprise, which I will now endeavour
to describe.

The first step in the real push—the step which
above all others was to count—was the night attack
on the summits of the Sari Bair ridge.   The crest
line of this lofty mountain range runs parallel to
the sea, dominating the under-features contained
within the Anzac position, although these fortunately defilade the actual landing-place.   From the
main ridge a series of spurs run down towards the
level beach, and are separated from one another
by deep, jagged gullies choked up with dense
jungle.   Two of these leading up to Chunuk Bair
are called Chailak Dere and Sazli Beit Dere;
another deep ravine runs up to Koja Chemen Tepe
(Hill 305), the topmost peak of the whole ridge,
and is called the Aghyl Dere.

ATTACKS BY STAGES

It was our object to effect a lodgment along the crest of the high main ridge with two columns of troops, but, seeing the nature of the ground and the dispositions of the enemy, the effort had to be made by stages. We were bound, in fact, to undertake a double subsidiary operation before we could hope to launch these attacks with any real prospect of success.

(1) The right covering force was to seize Table Top, as well as all other enemy positions commanding the foothills between the Chailak Dere and the Sazli Beit Dere ravines. If this enterprise succeeded it would open up the ravines for the assaulting columns, whilst at the same time interposing between the right flank of the left covering force and the enemy holding the Sari Bair main ridge.

(2) The left covering force was to march northwards along the beach to seize a hill called Damakjelik Bair, some 1,400 yards north of Table Top. If successful it would be able to hold out a hand to the 9th Corps as it landed south of Nibrunesi Point, whilst at the same time protecting the left flank of the left assaulting column against enemy troops from the Anafarta valley during its climb up the Aghyl Dere ravine.

(3) The right assaulting column was to move up the Chailak Dere and Sazli Beit Dere ravines to the storm of the ridge of Chunuk Bair.

(4) The left assaulting column was to work up the Aghyl Dere and prolong the line of the right assaulting column by storming Hill 305 (Koja Chemen Tepe), the summit of the whole range of hills.

To recapitulate, the two assaulting columns, which were to work up three ravines to the storm of the high ridge, were to be preceded by two covering columns. One of these was to capture the enemy's positions commanding the foothills, first to open the mouths of the ravines, secondly to cover the right flank of another covering force whilst it marched along the beach. The other covering column was to strike far out to the north until, from a hill called Damakjelik Bair, it could at the same time facilitate the landing of the 9th Corps at Nibrunesi Point, and guard the left flank of the column assaulting Sari Bair from any forces of the enemy which might be assembled in the Anafarta valley.

COMMANDING OFFICERS

The whole of this big attack was placed under the command of Major-General Sir A. J. Godley, General Officer Commanding New Zealand and Australian Division. The two covering and the two assaulting columns were organised as follows : —

Right Covering Column, under Brigadier-

General A. H. Russell.—New Zealand Mounted Rifles Brigade, the Otago Mounted Rifles Regiment, the Maori Contingent and New Zealand Field Troop.

Right Assaulting Column, under Brigadier-General F. E. Johnston.—New Zealand Infantry Brigade, Indian Mountain Battery (less one section), one Company New Zealand Engineers.

Left Covering Column, under Brigadier-General J. H. Travers.—Headquarters 40th Brigade, half the 72nd Field Company, 4th Battalion South Wales Borderers, and 5th Battalion Wiltshire Regiment.

Left Assaulting Column, under Brigadier-General (now Major-General) H. V. Cox.—29th Indian Infantry Brigade, 4th Australian Infantry Brigade, Indian Mountain Battery (less one section), one Company New Zealand Engineers.

Divisional Reserve.—6th Battalion South Lancashire Regiment and 8th Battalion Welsh Regiment (Pioneers) at Chailak Dere, and the 39th Infantry Brigade and half 72nd Field Company at Aghyl Dere.

The right covering column, it will be remembered, had to gain command of the Sazli Beit Dere and the Aghyl Dere ravines, so as to let the assaulting column arrive intact within striking distance of the Chunuk Bair ridge. To achieve this object it had to clear the Turks off from their right flank positions upon Old No. 3 Post and Table Top.

THE RAZOR-BACK CONNECTION

Old No. 3 Post, connected with Table Top by a razor back, formed the apex of a triangular piece of hill sloping gradually down to our No. 2 and No. 3 outposts. Since its recapture from us by the Turks on 30th May working parties had done their best with unstinted material to convert this commanding point into an impregnable redoubt. Two lines of fire trench, very heavily entangled, protected its southern face—the only one accessible to us—and, with its head cover of solid timber baulks and its strongly revetted outworks, it dominated the approaches of both the Chailak Dere and the Sazli Beit Dere.

Table Top is a steep-sided, flat-topped hill, close on 400 feet above sea level. The sides of the hill are mostly sheer and quite impracticable, but here and there a ravine, choked with scrub, and under fire of enemy trenches, gives precarious foothold up the precipitous cliffs. The small plateau on the summit was honeycombed with trenches, which were connected by a communication alley with that under-feature of Sari Bair known as Rhododendron Spur.

SUCCESSFUL STRATAGEMS

Amongst other stratagems the Anzac troops, assisted by H.M.S. *Colne*, had long and carefully

D

been educating the Turks how they should lose Old No. 3 Post, which could hardly have been rushed by simple force of arms. Every night, exactly at 9 p.m., H.M.S. *Colne* threw the beam of her searchlight on to the redoubt, and opened fire upon it for exactly ten minutes. Then, after a ten minutes' interval, came a second illumination and bombardment, commencing always at 9.20 and ending precisely at 9.30 p.m.

The idea was that, after successive nights of such practice, the enemy would get into the habit of taking the searchlight as a hint to clear out until the shelling was at an end. But on the eventful night of the 6th, the sound of their footsteps drowned by the loud cannonade, unseen as they crept along in that darkest shadow which fringes a searchlight's beam—came the right covering column. At 9.30 the light switched off, and instantly our men poured out of the scrub jungle and into the empty redoubt. By 11 p.m. the whole series of surrounding entrenchments were ours !

Once the capture of Old No. 3 Post was fairly under way, the remainder of the right covering column carried on with their attack upon Bauchop's Hill and the Chailak Dere. By 10 p.m. the northernmost point, with its machine-gun, was captured, and by 1 o'clock in the morning the whole of Bauchop's Hill, a maze of ridge and ravine, everywhere entrenched, was fairly in our hands.

Night Attacks

The attack along the Chailak Dere was not so cleanly carried out—made, indeed, just about as ugly a start as any enemy could wish. Pressing eagerly forward through the night, the little column of stormers found themselves held up by a barbed-wire erection of unexampled height, depth, and solidity, which completely closed the river bed—that is to say, the only practicable entrance to the ravine. The entanglement was flanked by a strongly held enemy trench running right across the opening of the Chailak Dere.

Here that splendid body of men, the Otago Mounted Rifles, lost some of their bravest and their best, but in the end, when things were beginning to seem desperate, a passage was forced through the stubborn obstacle with most conspicuous and cool courage by Captain Shera and a party of New Zealand Engineers, supported by the Maoris, who showed themselves worthy descendants of the warriors of the Gate Pah. Thus was the mouth of the Chailak Dere opened in time to admit of the unopposed entry of the right assaulting column.

Bravery and Valour

Simultaneously the attack on Table Top had been launched under cover of a heavy bombard-

ment from H.M.S. *Colne*. No General on peace
manœuvres would ask troops to attempt so break-
neck an enterprise. The flanks of Table Top are
so steep that the height gives an impression of a
mushroom shape—of the summit bulging out over
its stem. But just as faith moves mountains, so
valour can carry them. The Turks fought bravely.
The angle of Table Top's ascent is recognised in
our regulations as "impracticable for infantry."
But neither Turks nor angles of ascent were
destined to stop Russell or his New Zealanders
that night.

There are moments during battle when life becomes intensified, when men become supermen,
when the impossible becomes simple—and this was
one of those moments. The scarped heights were
scaled, the plateau was carried by midnight. With
this brilliant feat the task of the right covering
force was at an end. Its attacks had been made
with the bayonet and bomb only; magazines were
empty by order; hardly a rifle shot had been fired.
Some 150 prisoners were captured as well as many
rifles and much equipment, ammunition, and
stores. No words can do justice to the achievement of Brigadier-General Russell and his men.
There are exploits which must be seen to be
realised.

The right assaulting column had entered the
two southerly ravines—Sazli Beit Dere and Chailak
Dere—by midnight. At 1.30 a.m. began a hotly
contested fight for the trenches on the lower part
of Rhododendron Spur, whilst the Chailak Dere

column pressed steadily up the valley against the enemy.

The South Wales Borderers

The left covering column, under Brigadier-General Travers, after marching along the beach to No. 3 Outpost, resumed its northerly advance as soon as the attack on Bauchop's Hill had developed. Once the Chailak Dere was cleared the column moved by the mouth of the Aghyl Dere, disregarding the enfilade fire from sections of Bauchop's Hill still uncaptured. The rapid success of this movement was largely due to Lieutenant-Colonel Gillespie, a very fine man, who commanded the advance guard consisting of his own regiment, the 4th South Wales Borderers, a corps worthy of such a leader. Every trench encountered was instantly rushed by the Borderers until, having reached the predetermined spot, the whole column was unhesitatingly launched at Damakjelik Bair. Several Turkish trenches were captured at the bayonet's point, and by 1.30 a.m. the whole of the hill was occupied, thus safe-guarding the left rear of the whole of the Anzac attack.

Here was an encouraging sample of what the New Army, under good auspices, could accomplish. Nothing more trying to inexperienced troops can be imagined than a long night march exposed to flanking fire, through a strange country, winding up at the end with a bayonet charge against a height, formless and still in the starlight, garrisoned by those spectres of the imagination, worst enemies of the soldier.

TURKISH OFFICERS IN PYJAMAS

The left assaulting column crossed the Chailak Dere at 12.30 a.m., and entered the Aghyl Dere at the heels of the left covering column. The surprise, on this side, was complete. Two Turkish officers were caught in their pyjamas; enemy arms and ammunition were scattered in every direction.

The grand attack was now in full swing, but the country gave new sensations in cliff climbing even to officers and men who had graduated over the goat tracks of Anzac. The darkness of the night, the density of the scrub, hands and knees progress up the spurs, sheer physical fatigue, exhaustion of the spirit caused by repeated hairbreadth escapes from the hail of random bullets—all these combined to take the edge off the energies of our troops. At last, after advancing some distance up the Aghyl Dere, the column split up into two parts. The 4th Australian Brigade struggled, fighting hard as they went, up to the north of the northern fork of the Aghyl Dere, making for Hill 305 (Koja Chemen Tepe). The 29th Indian Infantry Brigade scrambled up the south fork of the Aghyl Dere and the spurs north of it to the attack of a portion of the Sari Bair ridge known as Hill Q.

A Marvellous Advance

Dawn broke and the crest line was not yet in our hands, although, considering all things, the left assaulting column had made a marvellous advance. The 4th Australian Infantry Brigade was on the line of the Asma Dere (the next ravine north of the Aghyl Dere), and the 29th Indian Infantry Brigade held the ridge west of the Farm below Chunuk Bair and along the spurs to the north-east. The enemy had been flung back from ridge to ridge; an excellent line for the renewal of the attack had been secured, and (except for the exhaustion of the troops) the auspices were propitious.

Turning to the right assaulting column, one battalion, the Canterbury Infantry Battalion, clambered slowly up the Sazli Beit Dere. The remainder of the force, led by the Otago Battalion, wound their way amongst the pitfalls and forced their passage through the scrub of the Chailak Dere, where fierce opposition forced them ere long to deploy. Here, too, the hopeless country was the main hindrance, and it was not until 5.45 a.m. that the bulk of the column joined the Canterbury Battalion on the lower slopes of Rhododendron Spur.

JUST SHORT OF VICTORY

The whole force then moved up the spur, gaining touch with the left assaulting column by means of the 10th Gurkhas, in face of very heavy fire and frequent bayonet charges. Eventually they entrenched on the top of Rhododendron Spur, a quarter of a mile short of Chunuk Bair—*i.e.*, of victory.

At 7.0 a.m. the 5th and 6th Gurkhas, belonging to the left assaulting column, had approached the main ridge north-east of Chunuk Bair, whilst, on their left, the 14th Sikhs had got into touch with the 4th Australian Brigade on the southern watershed of the Asmak Dere. The 4th Australian Brigade now received orders to leave half a battalion to hold the spur, and, with the rest of its strength, plus the 14th Sikhs, to assault Hill 305 (Koja Chemen Tepe). But by this time the enemy's opposition had hardened, and his reserves were moving up from the direction of Battleship Hill. Artillery support was asked for and given, yet by 9.0 a.m. the attack of the right assaulting column on Chunuk Bair was checked, and any idea of a further advance on Koja Chemen Tepe had to be, for the moment, suspended. The most that could be done was to hold fast to the Asmak Dere watershed whilst attacking the ridge north-east of Chunuk Bair, an attack to be supported by a fresh assault launched against Chunuk Bair itself.

MAP 3.

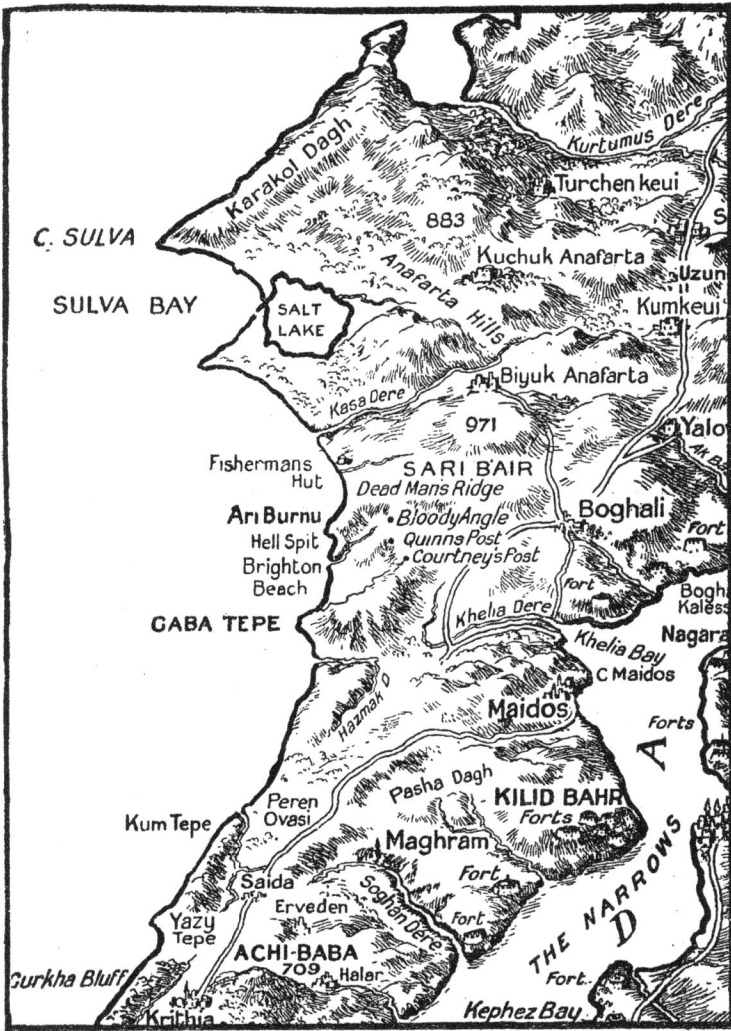

C. SULVA

SULVA BAY

Karakol Dagh

883

Kurtumus Dere

Turchen keui

Kuchuk Anafarta

Uzun

Anafarta Hills

Kumkeui

SALT
LAKE

Kasa Dere

Biyuk Anafarta

971

Yalo

Fishermans
Hut

SARI B'AIR
Dead Mans Ridge

Ak Ba

Ari Burnu

Bloody Angle

Boghali

Hell Spit
Brighton
Beach

Quinns Post
Courtney's Post

fort

Bogh
Kaless

GABA TEPE

Khelia Dere

fort

Khelia Bay

C Maidos

Nagara

Maidos

Forts

Hazmak D

Pasha Dagh

KILID BAHR

Peren
Ovasi

Forts

Kum Tepe

Maghram

Fort

Saida

Erveden

Soghan Dere

Fort

Yazy
Tepe

THE NARROWS

Gurkha Bluff

ACHI-BABA
709

Halar

D

Fort

Krithia

Kephez Bay

1   5   10

ON BATTLESHIP HILL

At 9.30 a.m. the two assaulting columns pressed forward whilst our guns pounded the enemy moving along the Battleship Hill spurs. But in spite of all their efforts their increasing exhaustion as opposed to the gathering strength of the enemy's fresh troops began to tell—they had shot their bolt. So all day they clung to what they had captured and strove to make ready for the night. At 11 a.m. three battalions of the 39th Infantry Brigade were sent up from the general reserve to be at hand when needed, and, at the same hour, one more battalion of the reserve was dispatched to the 1st Australian Division to meet the drain caused by all the desperate Lone Pine fighting.

By the afternoon the position of the two assaulting columns was unchanged. The right covering force were in occupation of Table Top, Old No. 3 Post, and Bauchop's Hill, which General Russell had been ordered to maintain with two regiments of Mounted Rifles, so that he might have two other regiments and the Maori Contingent available to move as required. The left covering force held Damakjelik Bair. The forces which had attacked along the front of the original Anzac line were back again in their own trenches. The Lone Pine work was being furiously disputed. All had suffered heavily and all were very tired.

A Feat "Without Parallel"

So ended the first phase of the fighting for the Chunuk Bair ridge. Our aims had not fully been attained, and the help we had hoped for from Suvla had not been forthcoming. Yet I fully endorse the words of General Birdwood when he says : "The troops had performed a feat which is without parallel."

Great kudos is due to Major-Generals Godley and Shaw for their arrangements; to Generals Russell, Johnston, Cox, and Travers for their leading; but most of all, as every one of these officers will gladly admit, to the rank and file for their fighting. Nor may I omit to add that the true destroyer spirit with which H.M.S. *Colne* (Commander Claude Seymour, R.N.) and H.M.S. *Chelmer* (Commander Hugh T. England, R.N.) backed us up will live in the grateful memories of the Army.

A Fresh Advance

In the course of this afternoon (7th August) reconnaissances of Sari Bair were carried out and the troops were got into shape for a fresh advance in three columns, to take place in the early morning.

The columns were composed as follows :—

Right Column, Brigadier-General F. E. Johnston.—26th Indian Mountain Battery (less one section), Auckland Mounted Rifles, New Zealand Infantry Brigade, two battalions 13th Division, and the Maori Contingent.

Centre and Left Columns, Major-General H. V. Cox.—21st Indian Mountain Battery (less one section), 4th Australian Brigade, 39th Infantry Brigade (less one battalion), with 6th Battalion South Lancashire Regiment attached, and the 29th Indian Infantry Brigade.

The right column was to climb up the Chunuk Bair ridge; the left column was to make for the prolongation of the ridge north-east to Koja Chemen Tepe, the topmost peak of the range.

The Summit Gained

The attack was timed for 4.15 a.m. At the first faint glimmer of dawn observers saw figures moving against the sky-line of Chunuk Bair. Were they our own men, or were they the Turks? Telescopes were anxiously adjusted; the light grew stronger; men were seen climbing up from our side of the ridge; they *were* our own fellows—the topmost summit was ours!

On the right General Johnston's column, headed by the Wellington Battalion and supported by the 7th Battalion Gloucestershire Regiment, the Auckland Mounted Rifles Regiment, the 8th Welsh Pioneers, and the Maori Contingent, the whole most gallantly led by Lieutenant-Colonel W. G. Malone, had raced one another up the steep. Nothing could check them.   On they went, until, with a last determined rush, they fixed themselves firmly on the south-western slopes and crest of the main knoll known as the height of Chunuk Bair.   With deep regret I have to add that the brave Lieutenant-Colonel Malone fell mortally wounded as he was marking out the line to be held.

The 7th Gloucesters suffered terrible losses here. The fire was so hot that they never got a chance to dig their trenches deeper than some six inches, and there they had to withstand attack after attack. In the course of these fights every single officer, company sergeant-major, or company quarter-master-sergeant was either killed or wounded, and the battalion by midday consisted of small groups of men commanded by junior non-commissioned officers or privates.

"A Soldiers' Battle"

Chapter and verse may be quoted for the view that the rank-and-file of an army cannot long endure the strain of close hand-to-hand fighting unless they are given confidence by the example of good officers.   Yet here is at least one instance where a battalion of the New Army fought right on, from midday till sunset, without *any* officers.

In the centre the 39th Infantry Brigade and the 29th Indian Brigade moved along the gullies leading up to the Sari Bair ridge—the right moving south of the Farm on Chunuk Bair, the left up the spurs to the north-east of the Farm against a portion of the main ridge north-east of Chunuk Bair, and the col to the north of it. So murderous was the enemy's fire that little progress could be made, though some ground was gained on the spurs to the north-east of the Farm.

AUSTRALIANS AT BAY

On the left the 4th Australian Brigade advanced from the Asmak Dere against the lower slopes of Abdul Rahman Bair (a spur running due north from Koja Chemen Tepe) with the intention of wheeling to its right and advancing up the spur. Cunningly placed Turkish machine-guns and a strong entrenched body of infantry were ready for this move, and the Brigade were unable to get on. At last, on the approach of heavy columns of the enemy, the Australians, virtually surrounded, and having already suffered losses of over 1,000, were withdrawn to their original position. Here they stood at bay, and, though the men were by now half-dead with thirst and with fatigue, they bloodily repulsed attack after attack delivered by heavy columns of Turks.

REPULSED, BUT UNDEFEATED

So stood matters at noon. Enough had been done for honour and much ground had everywhere been gained. The expected support from Suvla hung fire, but the capture of Chunuk Bair was a presage of victory; even the troops who had been repulsed were quite undefeated—quite full of fight —and so it was decided to hold hard as we were till nightfall, and then to essay one more grand attack, wherein the footing gained on Chunuk Bair would this time be used as a pivot.

In the afternoon the battle slackened, excepting always at Lone Pine, where the enemy were still coming on in mass, and being mown down by our fire. Elsewhere the troops were busy digging and getting up water and food, no child's play, with their wretched lines of communication running within musketry range of the enemy.

That evening the New Zealand Brigade, with two regiments of New Zealand Mounted Rifles and the Maoris, held Rhododendron Spur and the south-western slopes of the main knoll of Chunuk Bair. The front line was prolonged by the columns of General Cox and General Monash (with the 4th Australian Brigade). Behind the New Zealanders were the 38th Brigade in reserve, and in rear of General Monash two battalions of the 40th Brigade. The inner line was held as before, and the 29th Brigade (less two battalions) had been sent up from the general reserve, and remained still further in rear.

COMPOSITION OF THE COLUMNS

The columns for the renewed attack were composed as follows :—

No. 1 Column, Brigadier-General F. E. Johnston.—26th Indian Mountain Battery (less one section), the Auckland and Wellington Mounted Rifles Regiments, the New Zealand Infantry Brigade, and two battalions of the 13th Division.

No. 2 Column, Major-General H. V. Cox.—21st Indian Mountain Battery (less one section), 4th Australian Brigade, 39th Brigade (less the 7th Gloucesters, relieved), with the 6th Battalion South Lancashire Regiment attached, and the Indian Infantry Brigade.

No. 3 Column, Brigadier-General A. H. Baldwin, Commanding 38th Infantry Brigade.—Two battalions each from the 38th and 29th Brigades and one from the 40th Brigade.

No. 1 column was to hold and consolidate the ground gained on the 6th, and, in co-operation with the other columns, to gain the whole of Chunuk Bair, and extend to the south-east. No. 2 column was to attack Hill Q on the Chunuk Bair ridge, and No. 3 column was to move from the Chailak Dere, also on Hill Q. This last column was to make the main attack, and the others were to co-operate with it.

A Mass of Flame and Smoke

At 4.30 a.m. on 9th August the Chunuk Bair ridge and Hill Q were heavily shelled. The naval guns, all the guns on the left flank, and as many as possible from the right flank (whence the enemy's advance could be enfiladed), took part in this cannonade, which rose to its climax at 5.15 a.m., when the whole ridge seemed a mass of flame and smoke, whence huge clouds of dust drifted slowly upwards in strange patterns on to the sky. At 5.16 a.m. this tremendous bombardment was to be switched off on to the flanks and reverse slopes of the heights.

General Baldwin's column had assembled in the Chailak Dere, and was moving up towards General Johnston's headquarters. Our plan contemplated the massing of this column immediately behind the trenches held by the New Zealand Infantry Brigade. Thence it was intended to launch the battalions in successive lines, keeping them as much as possible on the high ground.

DARKNESS AND AWFUL COUNTRY

Infinite trouble had been taken to ensure that the narrow track should be kept clear; guides also were provided; but in spite of all precautions the darkness, the rough scrub-covered country, its sheer steepness, so delayed the column that they were unable to take full advantage of the configuration of the ground, and, inclining to the left, did not reach the line of the Farm—Chunuk Bair till 5.15 a.m. In plain English, Baldwin, owing to the darkness and the awful country, lost his way— through no fault of his own. The mischance was due to the fact that time did not admit of the

E

detailed careful reconnaissance of routes which is so essential where operations are to be carried out by night.

And now, under that fine leader, Major C. G. L. Allanson, the 6th Gurkhas of the 29th Indian Infantry Brigade pressed up the slopes of Sari Bair, crowned the heights of the col between Chunuk Bair and Hill Q, viewed far beneath them the waters of the Hellespont, viewed the Asiatic shores along which motor transport was bringing supplies to the lighters. Not only did this battalion, as well as some of the 6th South Lancashire Regiment, reach the crest, but they began to attack down the far side of it, firing as they went at the fast retreating enemy. But the fortune of war was against us.

A Salvo of Heavy Shell

At this supreme moment Baldwin's column was still a long way from our trenches on the crest of Chunuk Bair, whence they should even now have been sweeping out towards Q along the whole ridge of the mountain. And instead of Baldwin's support came suddenly a salvo of heavy shell. These falling so unexpectedly among the stormers threw them into terrible confusion. The Turkish commander saw his chance; instantly his troops were rallied and brought back in a counter-charge, and the South Lancashires and Gurkhas, who had seen the promised land and had seemed for a moment to have held victory in their grasp, were forced backwards over the crest and on to the lower slopes whence they had first started.

But where was the main attack—where was Baldwin? When that bold but unlucky commander found he could not possibly reach our trenches on the top of Chunuk Bair in time to take effective part in the fight he deployed for attack where he stood, *i.e.*, at the farm to the left of the New Zealand Brigade's trenches on Rhododendron Spur. Now his men were coming on in fine style, and just as the Turks topped the ridge with shouts of elation, two companies of the 6th East Lancashire Regiment, together with the 10th Hampshire Regiment, charged up our side of the slope with the bayonet. They had gained the high ground immediately below the commanding knoll on Chunuk Bair, and a few minutes earlier would have joined hands with the Gurkhas and South Lancashires and, combined with them, would have carried all before them.

New Army's Audacity

But the Turks by this time were lining the whole of the high crest in overwhelming numbers. The New Army troops attacked with a fine audacity, but they were flung back from the height and then pressed still further down the slope, until General Baldwin had to withdraw his command to the vicinity of the Farm, whilst the enemy, much encouraged, turned their attention to the New Zealand troops and the two New Army battalions of No. 1 column still holding the south-west half of the main knoll of Chunuk Bair. Constant attacks, urged with fanatical persistence, were met here with a sterner resolution, and although, at the end of the day, our troops were greatly exhausted, they still kept their footing on the summit. And if that summit meant much to us, it meant even more to the Turks. For the ridge covered our landing-places, it is true, but it covered not only the Turkish beaches at Kilia Leman and Maidos, but also the Narrows themselves and the roads leading northward to Bulair and Constantinople.

SHALLOW TRENCHES

That evening our line ran along Rhododendron Spur up to the crest of Chunuk Bair, where about 200 yards were occupied and held by some 800 men. Slight trenches had hastily been dug, but the fatigue of the New Zealanders and the fire of the enemy had prevented solid work being done. The trenches in many places were not more than a few inches deep. They were not protected by wire. Also many officers are of opinion that they had not been well sited in the first instance. On the South African system the main line was withdrawn some twenty-five yards from the crest instead of being actually on the crest-line itself, and there were not even look-out posts along the summit. Boer skirmishers would thus have had to show themselves against the skyline before they could annoy. But here we were faced by regulars taught to attack in mass with bayonet or bomb. And the power of collecting overwhelming numbers at very close quarters rested with whichever side held the true skyline in force.

From Chunuk Bair the line ran down to the Farm and almost due north to the Asmak Dere southern watershed, whence it continued westward to the sea near Asmak Kuyu. On the right the Australian Division was still holding its line and Lone Pine was still being furiously attacked. The 1st Australian Brigade was now reduced from 2,900 to 1,000, and the total casualties up to 8 p.m. on the 9th amounted to about 8,500. But the troops were still in extraordinarily good heart, and nothing could damp their keenness. The only discontent shown was by men who were kept in reserve.

THREE DAYS AND NIGHTS FIGHTING

During the night of the 9th-10th, the New Zealand and New Army troops on Chunuk Bair were relieved. For three days and three nights they had been ceaselessly fighting. They were half-dead with fatigue. Their lines of communication, started from sea level, ran across trackless ridges and ravines to an altitude of 800 ft., and were exposed all the way to snipers' fire and artillery bombardment. It had become imperative, therefore, to get them enough food, water, and rest; and for this purpose it was imperative also to withdraw them. Chunuk Bair, which they had so magnificently held, was now handed over to two battalions of the 13th Division, which were connected by the 10th Hampshire Regiment with the troops at the farm. General Sir William Birdwood is emphatic on the point that the nature of the ground is such that there was no room on the crest for more than this body of 800 to 1,000 rifles.

Strengthening the Defences

The two battalions of the New Army chosen to hold Chunuk Bair were the 6th Loyal North Lancashire Regiment and the 5th Wiltshire Regiment. The first of these arrived in good time and occupied the trenches.

Even in the darkness their commanding officer, Lieutenant-Colonel Levinge, recognised how dangerously these trenches were sited, and he began at once to dig observation posts on the actual crest and to strengthen the defences where he could. But he had not time given him to do much. The second battalion, the Wiltshires, were delayed by the intricate country. They did not reach the edge of the entrenchment until 4 a.m., and were then told to lie down in what was believed, erroneously, to be a covered position.

At daybreak on Tuesday, 10th August, the Turks delivered a grand attack from the line Chunuk Bair—Hill Q against these two battalions, already weakened in numbers, though not in spirit, by previous fighting. First our men were shelled by every enemy gun, and then, at 5.30 a.m., were assaulted by a huge column, consisting of no less than a full division plus a regiment of three battalions.

NORTH LANCASHIRES OVERWHELMED

The North Lancashire men were simply overwhelmed in their shallow trenches by sheer weight of numbers, whilst the Wilts, who were caught out in the open, were literally almost annihilated. The ponderous mass of the enemy swept over the crest, turned the right flank of our line below, swarmed round the Hampshires and General Baldwin's column, which had to give ground, and were only extricated with great difficulty and very heavy losses.

THE CHANCE OF A LIFETIME

Now it was our turn. The warships and the New Zealand and Australian Artillery, the Indian Mountain Artillery Brigade, and the 69th Brigade

Royal Field Artillery were getting the chance of a lifetime. As the successive solid lines of Turks topped the crest of the ridge gaps were torn through their formation, and an iron rain fell on them as they tried to re-form in the gullies.

Not here only did the Turks pay dearly for their recapture of the vital crest. Enemy reinforcements continued to move up Battleship Hill under heavy and accurate fire from our guns, and still they kept topping the ridges and pouring down the western slopes of the Chunuk Bair as if determined to regain everything they had lost. But once they were over the crest they became exposed not only to the full blast of the guns, naval and military, but also to a battery of ten machine-guns belonging to the New Zealand Infantry Brigade, which played upon their serried ranks at close range until the barrels were red hot. Enormous losses were inflicted, especially by these ten machine-guns; and, of the swarms which had once fairly crossed the crest-line, only the merest handful ever straggled back to their own side of Chunuk Bair.

At this same time strong forces of the enemy (forces which I had reckoned would have been held back to meet our advance from Suvla Bay) were hurled against the Farm and the spurs to the north-east, where there arose a conflict so deadly that it may be considered as the climax of the four days' fighting for the ridge.

"Caught One Another by the Throat"

Portions of our line were pierced, and the troops driven clean down the hill. At the foot of the hill the men were rallied by Staff-Captain Street, who was there supervising the transport of food and water. Without a word, unhesitatingly, they followed him back to the Farm, where they plunged again into the midst of that series of struggles in which generals fought in the ranks and men dropped their scientific weapons and caught one another by the throat. So desperate a battle cannot be described.

Died Where They Stood

The Turks came on again and again, fighting magnificently, calling upon the name of God. Our men stood to it, and maintained, by many a deed of daring, the old traditions of their race. There was no flinching. They died in the ranks where they stood. Here Generals Cayley, Baldwin, and Cooper and all their gallant men achieved great glory. On this bloody field fell Brigadier-General Baldwin, who earned his first laurels on Cæsar's Camp at Ladysmith. There, too, fell Brigadier-General Cooper, badly wounded; and there, too, fell Lieutenant-Colonel M. H. Nunn, commanding the 9th Worcestershire Regiment; Lieutenant-Colonel H. G. Levinge, commanding the 6th Loyal North Lancashire Regiment; and Lieutenant-Colonel J. Carden, commanding the 5th Wiltshire Regiment.

"THE LAST TWO BATTALIONS"

Towards this supreme struggle the absolute last two battalions from the General Reserve were now hurried, but by 10.0 a.m. the effort of the enemy was spent. Soon their shattered remnants began to trickle back, leaving a track of corpses behind them, and by night, except prisoners or wounded, no live Turk was left upon our side of the slope.

That same day, 10th August, two attacks, one in the morning and the other in the afternoon, were delivered on our positions along the Asmak Dere and Damakjelik Bair. Both were repulsed with heavy loss by the 4th Australian Brigade and the 4th South Wales Borderers, the men of the New Army showing all the steadiness of veterans. Sad to say, the Borderers lost their intrepid leader, Lieutenant-Colonel Gillespie, in the course of this affair.

HEAVY LOSSES

By evening the total casualties of General Birdwood's force had reached 12,000, and included a very large proportion of officers. The 13th Division of the New Army, under Major-General Shaw, had alone lost 6,000 out of a grand total of

10,500. Baldwin was gone, and all his staff. Ten commanding officers out of thirteen had disappeared from the fighting effectives. The Warwicks and the Worcesters had lost literally every single officer. The old German notion that no unit would stand a loss of more than 25 per cent. had been completely falsified.

The 13th Division and the 29th Brigade of the 10th (Irish) Division had lost more than twice that proportion, and, in spirit, were game for as much more fighting as might be required. But physically, though Birdwood's forces were prepared to hold all they had got, they were now too exhausted to attack—at least until they had rested and reorganised.

So far they *had* held on to all they had gained, excepting only the footholds on the ridge between Chunuk Bair and Hill Q, momentarily carried by the Gurkhas, and the salient of Chunuk Bair itself, which they had retained for forty-eight hours. Unfortunately, these two pieces of ground, small and worthless as they seemed, were worth, according to the ethics of war, 10,000 lives, for by their loss or retention they just marked the difference between an important success and a signal victory.

WATER TROUBLES ONCE MORE

At times I had thought of throwing my reserves into this stubborn central battle, where probably they would have turned the scale. But each time the water troubles made me give up the idea, all ranks at Anzac being reduced to one pint a day. True thirst is a sensation unknown to the dwellers in cool, well-watered England. But at Anzac, when mules with water "pakhals" arrived at the front, the men would rush up to them in swarms, just to lick the moisture that had exuded through the canvas bags. It will be understood, then, that until wells had been discovered under the freshly won hills the reinforcing of Anzac by even so much as a brigade was unthinkable.

The grand *coup* had not come off. The Narrows were still out of sight and beyond field-gun range. But this was not the fault of Lieutenant-General Birdwood or any of the officers and men under his command. No mortal can command success; Lieutenant-General Birdwood had done all that mortal man can do to deserve it. The way in which he worked out his instructions into practical arrangements and dispositions upon the terrain reflects high credit upon his military capacity.

I also wish to bring to your Lordship's notice the valuable services of Major-General Godley, commanding the New Zealand and Australian Division. He had under him at one time a force amounting to two divisions, which he handled with conspicuous ability. Major-General F. C. Shaw, commanding 13th Division, also rose superior to all the trials and tests of these trying days. His calm and sound judgment proved to be of the greatest value throughout the arduous fighting I have recorded.

UNBOUNDED ADMIRATION FOR THE TROOPS

As for the troops, the joyous alacrity with which they faced danger, wounds, and death, as if they were some new form of exciting recreation, has astonished me—old campaigner as I am. I will say no more, leaving Major-General Godley to speak for what happened under his eyes:—"I cannot close my report," he says, "without placing on record my unbounded admiration of the work performed, and the gallantry displayed, by the troops and their leaders during the severe fighting involved in these operations. Though the Australian, New Zealand, and Indian units had been confined to trench duty in a cramped space for some four months, and though the troops of the New Armies had only just landed from a sea voyage, and many of them had not been previously under fire, I do not believe that any troops in the world could have accomplished more. All ranks vied with one another in the performance of gallant deeds, and more than worthily upheld the best traditions of the British Army."

Although the Sari Bair ridge was the key to the whole of my tactical conception, and although the temptation to view this vital Anzac battle at closer quarters was very hard to resist, there was nothing

in its course or conduct to call for my personal
intervention.

SUVLA BAY OPERATIONS

GENERAL STOPFORD IN COMMAND

The conduct of the operations which were to be
based upon Suvla Bay was entrusted to Lieutenant-
General the Hon. Sir F. Stopford. At his
disposal was placed the 9th Army Corps, less the
13th Division and the 29th Brigade of the 10th
Division.

We believed that the Turks were still unsus-
picious about Suvla and that their only defences
near that part of the coast were a girdle of trenches
round Lala Baba and a few unconnected lengths
of fire trench on Hill 10 and on the hills forming
the northern arm of the bay. There was no
wire. Inland a small work had been con-
structed on Yilghin Burnu (locally known as
Chocolate Hills), and a few guns had been placed
upon these hills, as well as upon Ismail Oglu
Tepe, whence they could be brought into action
either against the beaches of Suvla Bay or
against any attempt from Anzac to break
out northwards and attack Chunuk Bair.

ACCURACY OF INTELLIGENCE DEPARTMENT

The numbers of the enemy allotted for the defence of the Suvla and Ejelmer areas (including the troops in the Anafarta villages, but exclusive of the general reserves in rear of the Sari Bair) were supposed to be under 4,000. Until the Turkish version of these events is in our hands it is not possible to be certain of the accuracy of this estimate. All that can be said at present is that my Intelligence Department were wonderfully exact in their figures as a rule and that, in the case in question, events, the reports made by prisoners, etc., etc., seem to show that the forecast was correct.

Arrangements for the landing of the 9th Corps at Suvla were worked out in minute detail by my General Headquarters Staff in collaboration with the staff of Vice-Admiral de Robeck, and every precaution was taken to ensure that the destination of the troops was kept secret up to the last moment.

11TH DIVISION FERRIED OVER

Whilst concentrated at the island of Imbros the spirit and physique of the 11th Division had impressed me very favourably. They were to lead off the landing. From Imbros they were to be ferried over to the Peninsula in destroyers and motor-lighters. Disembarkation was to begin at 10.30 p.m., half an hour later than the attack on the Turkish outposts on the northern flank at Anzac, and I was sanguine enough to hope that the elaborate plan we had worked out would enable three complete brigades of infantry to be set ashore by daylight.

Originally it had been intended that all three brigades should land on the beach immediately south of Nibrunesi Point, but in deference to the representation of the Corps Commander I agreed, unfortunately, as it turned out, to one brigade being landed inside the bay.

The first task of the 9th Corps was to seize and hold the Chocolate and Ismail Oglu Hills, together with the high ground on the north and east of Suvla Bay. If the landing went off smoothly, and if my information regarding the strength of the enemy were correct, I hoped that these hills, with their guns, might be well in our possession before daybreak. In that case I hoped, further, that the first division which landed would be strong enough to picket and hold all the important heights within artillery range of the bay, when General Stopford would be able to direct the remainder of his force, as it became available, through the Anafartas to the east of the Sari Bair, where it should soon smash the mainspring of the Turkish opposition to Anzacs.

SECRET INSTRUCTIONS

On the 22nd July I issued secret instructions and tables showing the number of craft available for the 9th Corps commander, their capacity, and the points whereat the troops could be disembarked; also what numbers of troops, animals, vehicles, and stores could be landed simultaneously. The allocation of troops to the ships and boats was left to General Stopford's own discretion, subject only to naval exigencies, otherwise the order of the disembarkation might not have tallied with the order of his operations.

The factors governing the hour of landing were : First, that no craft could quit Kephalos Bay before dark (about 9 p.m.); secondly, that nothing could be done which would attract the attention of the enemy before 10 p.m., the moment when the outposts on the left flank of the Anzac position were to be rushed.

General Stopford next framed his orders on these secret instructions, and after they had received my complete approval he proceeded to expound them to the general officer commanding 11th Division and general officer commanding 10th Division, who came over from Mudros for the purpose.

LANDING FAVOURED BY WEATHER

As in the original landing, the luck of calm weather favoured us, and all the embarkation

F

arrangements at Kephalos were carried out by the Royal Navy in their usual ship-shape style. The 11th Division was to be landed at three places, designated and shown on the map as A, B, and C. Destroyers were told off for these landing-places, each destroyer towing a steam-lighter and picket-boat. Every light was to be dowsed, and as they neared the shore the destroyers were to slip their motor-lighters and picket-boats, which would then take the beach and discharge direct on to it.

The motor-lighters were new acquisitions since the first landing, and were to prove of the greatest possible assistance. They moved five knots an hour under their own engines, and carried 500 men, as well as stores of ammunition and water. After landing their passengers they were to return to the destroyers, and in one trip would empty them also. Ketches with service launches and transport lifeboats were to follow the destroyers and anchor at the entrance of the bay, so that in case of accidents or delays to any one of the motor-lighters a picket-boat could be sent at once to a ketch to pick up a tow of lifeboats and take the place of a disabled motor-lighter. These ketches and tows were afterwards to be used for evacuating the wounded.

CRUISERS AS TRANSPORTS

H.M.S. *Endymion* and H.M.S. *Theseus,* each carrying a thousand men, were also to sail from

Imbros after the destroyers, and, lying off the beach, were to discharge their troops directly the motor-lighters—three to each ship—were ready to convey the men to the shore, *i.e.,* after they had finished disembarking their own loads and those of the destroyers. When this was done—*i.e.,* after three trips—the motor-lighters would be free to go on transporting guns, stores, mules, etc.

The following crafts brought up the rear : —

(1) Two ketches, each towing four horse-boats carrying four 18-pounder guns and twenty-four horses.

(2) One ketch, towing horse-boats with forty horses.

(3) The sloop *Aster,* with 500 men, towing a lighter containing eight mountain guns.

(4) Three ketches, towing horse-boats containing eight 18-pounder guns and seventy-six horses.

Water-lighters, towed by a tank steamer, were also timed to arrive at A beach at daylight. When they had been emptied they were to return at once to Kephalos to refill from the parent water-ship.

THE "PRAH"

A specially fitted-out steamer, the *Prah,* with stores (shown by our experience of 25th April to be most necessary)—*i.e.,* water-pumps, hose, tanks, troughs, entrenching tools, and all ordnance stores requisite for the prompt development of wells or springs—was also sent to Suvla.

So much detail I have felt bound, for the sake of clearness, to give in the body of my despatch. The further detail, showing numbers landed, etc., etc., will be found in the appendix and tables to be issued later.

ORGANISING THE WATER SUPPLY

When originally I conceived the idea of these operations, one of the first points to be weighed was that of the water supply in the Biyuk Anafarta valley and the Suvla plain. Experience at Anzac had shown quite clearly that the whole plan must be given up unless a certain amount of water could be counted upon, and, fortunately, the information I received was reassuring. But, in case of accidents, and to be on the safe side, so long ago as June had I begun to take steps to counter the chance that we might, from one cause or another, find difficulty in developing the wells.

Having got from the War Office all that they could give me, I addressed myself to India and Egypt, and eventually from these three sources I managed to secure portable receptacles for 100,000 gallons, including petrol tins, milk cans, camel tanks, water bags, and pakhals.

LIGHTERS AND WATER-SHIPS

Supplementing these were lighters and water-ships, all under naval control. Indeed, by arrangement with the Admiral, the responsibility of the

MAP 4.

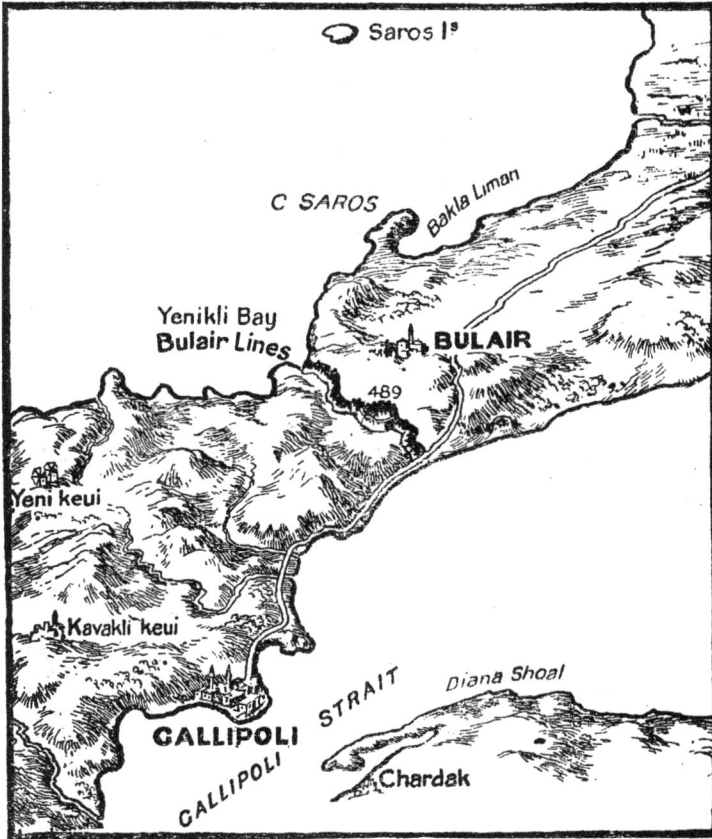

Army was confined to the emptying of the lighters and the distribution of the water to the troops, the Navy undertaking to bring the full lighters tc the shore to replace the empty ones, thus providing a continuous supply.

Finally 3,700 mules, together with 1,750 water carts, were provided for Anzac and Suvla—this in addition to 950 mules already at Anzac. Representatives of the Director of Supplies and Transport at Suvla and Anzac were sent to allot the transport which was to be used for carrying up whatever was most needed by units ashore, whether water, food, or ammunition.

This statement, though necessarily brief, will, I hope, suffice to throw some light upon the complexity of the arrangements thought out beforehand in order, so far as was humanly possible, to combat the disorganisation, the hunger and thirst which lie in wait for troops landing on a hostile beach.

On the evening of 6th August the 11th Division sailed on its short journey from Imbros (Kephalos) to Suvla Bay, and, meeting with no mischance, the landing took place, the brigades of the 11th Division getting ashore practically simultaneously; the 32nd and 33rd Brigades at B and C beaches, the 34th at A beach.

Turks Taken by Surprise

The surprise of the Turks was complete. At B and C the beaches were found to be admirably suited to their purpose, and there was no opposition. The landing at A was more difficult, both because of the shoal water and because there the Turkish pickets and sentries—the normal guardians of the coast—were on the alert and active. Some of the lighters grounded a good way from the shore, and men had to struggle towards the beach in as much as four feet six inches of water. Ropes in several instances were carried from the lighters to the shore to help to sustain the heavily accoutred infantry.

To add to the difficulties of the 34th Brigade the lighters came under flanking rifle fire from the Turkish outposts at Lala Baba and Ghazi Baba. The enemy even, knowing every inch of the ground, crept down in the very dark night on to the beach itself, mingling with our troops and getting between our firing line and its supports.

Fortunately the number of these enterprising foes was but few, and an end was soon put to their activity on the actual beaches by the sudden storming of Lala Baba from the south. This attack was carried out by the 9th West Yorkshire Regiment and the 6th Yorkshire Regiment, both of the 32nd Brigade, which had landed at B beach and marched up along the coast. The assault succeeded at once and without much loss, but both battalions deserve great credit for the way it was delivered in the inky darkness of the night.

The Manchesters' Good Work

The 32nd Brigade was now pushed on to the support of the 34th Brigade, which was held up by another outpost of the enemy on Hill 10 (117 R and S), and it is feared that some of the losses incurred here were due to misdirected fire. While this fighting was still in progress the 11th Battalion Manchester Regiment, of the 34th Brigade, was advancing northwards in very fine style, driving the enemy opposed to them back along the ridge of the Karakol Dagh towards the Kiretch Tepe Sirt. Beyond doubt these Lancashire men earned much distinction, fighting with great pluck and grit against an enemy not very numerous perhaps, but having an immense advantage in knowledge of the ground. As they got level with Hill 10 it grew light enough to see, and the enemy began to shell. No one seems to have been present who could take hold of the two brigades, the 32nd and 34th, and launch them in a concerted and cohesive attack. Consequently there were confusion and hesitation, increased by gorse fires lit by hostile shell, but redeemed, I am proud to report, by the conspicuously fine, soldierly conduct of several individual battalions.

The whole of the Turks locally available were by now in the field, and they were encouraged to counter-attack by the signs of hesitation, but the 9th Lancashire Fusiliers and the 11th Manchester Regiment took them on with the bayonet, and fairly drove them back in disorder over the flaming Hill 10.

As the infantry were thus making good, the two Highland mountain batteries and one battery, 59th Brigade, Royal Field Artillery, were landed at B beach. Day was now breaking, and with the dawn sailed into the bay six battalions of the 10th Division, under Brigadier-General Hill, from Mitylene.

Gratitude to the Navy

Here, perhaps, I may be allowed to express my gratitude to the Royal Navy for their share in this remarkable achievement, as well as a very natural pride at Staff arrangements, which resulted in the infantry of a whole division and three batteries being landed during a single night on a hostile shore, whilst the arrival of the first troops of the supporting division, from another base distant 120 miles, took place at the very psychological moment when support was most needed, namely, at break of dawn.

The intention of the Corps Commander was to keep the 10th Division on the left, and with it to push on as far forward as possible along the Kiretch Tepe Sirt towards the heights above Ejelmer Bay. He wished, therefore, to land these six battalions of the 10th Division at A beach, and, seeing Brigadier-General Hill, he told him that as the left of the 34th Brigade was being hard pressed he should get into touch with General Officer Commanding 11th Division, and work in support of his left until the arrival of his own Divisional General. But the Naval authorities, so General Stopford reports, were unwilling, for some reason not specified, to land these troops at A beach, so that they had to be sent in lighters to C beach, whence they marched by Lala Baba to Hill 10, under fire. Hence were caused loss, delay, and fatigue. Also the angle of direction from which these fresh troops entered the fight was not nearly so effective.

LANDING NEAR GHAZI BABA

The remainder of the 10th Division, three battalions (from Mudros), and with them the G.O.C., Lieutenant-General Sir B. Mahon, began to arrive, and the Naval authorities having discovered a suitable landing-place near Ghazi Baba, these battalions were landed there, together with one battalion of the 31st Brigade, which had not yet been sent round to C beach. By this means it was hoped that both the brigades of the 10th Division would be able to rendezvous about half a mile to the north-west of Hill 10.

After the defeat of the enemy round and about Hill 10, they retreated in an easterly direction towards Sulajik and Kuchuk Anafarta Ova, followed by the 34th and 32nd Brigades of the 11th Division and by the 31st Brigade of the 10th

Division, which had entered into the fight, not, as the Corps Commander had intended, on the left of the 11th Division, but between Hill 10 and the Salt Lake.

I have failed in my endeavours to get some live human detail about the fighting which followed, but I understand from the Corps Commander that the brunt of it fell upon the 31st Brigade of the 10th (Irish) Division, which consisted of the 6th Royal Inniskilling Fusiliers, the 6th Royal Irish Fusiliers, and the 6th Royal Dublin Fusiliers, the last-named battalion being attached to the 31st Brigade.

CHOCOLATE HILLS SEIZED

By the evening General Hammersley had seized Yilghin Burnu (Chocolate Hills) after a fight for which he specially commends the 6th Lincoln Regiment and the 6th Border Regiment. At the same time he reported that he was unable to ma'ke any further progress towards the vital point, Ismail Oglu Tepe. At nightfall his brigade and the 31st Brigade were extended from about Hetman Chair through Chocolate Hills, Sulajik, to near Kuchuk Anafarta Ova.

This same day Sir B. Mahon delivered a spirited attack along the Kiretch Tepe Sirt ridge, in support of the 11th Battalion Manchester Regiment, and, taking some small trenches *en route,* secured and established himself on a position extending

from the sea about 135 p., through the high ground
about the p. of Kiretch Tepe Sirt, to about 135 Z. 8.
In front of him, on the ridge, he reported the
enemy to be strongly entrenched. The 6th
Royal Munster Fusiliers have been named as
winning special distinction here. The whole
advance was well carried out by the Irishmen
over difficult ground against an enemy—500 to
700 Gendarmerie—favoured by the lie of the
land.

No Water

The weather was very hot, and the new troops
suffered much from want of water. Except at the
southernmost extremity of the Kiretch Tepe Sirt
ridge there was no water in that part of the field,
and although it existed in some abundance
throughout the area over which the 11th Division
was operating, the Corps Commander reports that
there was no time to develop its resources. Partly
this seems to have been owing to the enemy's fire;
partly to a want of that *nous* which stands by as
second nature to the old campaigner; partly it was
inevitable. Anyway, for as long as such a state of
things lasted, the troops became dependent on the
lighters and upon the water brought to the beaches
in tins, pakhals, etc.

Undoubtedly the distribution of this water to
the advancing troops was a matter of great difficulty, and one which required not only well-

worked-out schemes from Corps and Divisional
Staffs, but also energy and experience on the part
of those who had to put them into practice. As it
turned out, and judging merely by results, I
regret to say that the measures actually taken in
regard to the distribution proved to be inadequate, and that suffering and disorganisation ensued. The disembarkation of artillery
horses was therefore at once, and rightly,
postponed by the Corps Commander, in order
that mules might be landed to carry up
water.

Exhausted Men

And now General Stopford, recollecting the vast
issues which hung upon his success in forestalling
the enemy, urged his Divisional Commanders to
push on. Otherwise, as he saw, all the advantages
of the surprise landing must be nullified. But
the Divisional Commanders believed themselves,
it seems, to be unable to move. Their men, they
said, were exhausted by their efforts of the night
of the 6th-7th and by the action of the 7th. The
want of water had told on the new troops. The
distribution from the beaches had not worked
smoothly. In some cases the hose had been
pierced by individuals wishing to fill their own
bottles; in others lighters had grounded so far
from the beach that men swam out to fill batches
of water-bottles. All this had added to the dis-

organisation inevitable after a night landing, followed by fights here and there with an enemy scattered over a country to us unknown.

These pleas for delay were perfectly well-founded. But it seems to have been overlooked that the half-defeated Turks in front of us were equally exhausted and disorganised, and that an advance was the simplest and swiftest method of solving the water trouble and every other sort of trouble. Be this as it may, the objections overbore the Corps Commander's resolution. He had now got ashore three batteries (two of them mountain batteries), and the great guns of the ships were ready to speak at his request.

THE ROOT OF OUR FAILURE

But it was lack of artillery support which finally decided him to acquiesce in a policy of going slow which, by the time it reached the troops, became translated into a period of inaction. The Divisional Generals were, in fact, informed that, "in view of the inadequate artillery support," General Stopford did not wish them to make frontal attacks on entrenched positions, but desired them, so far as was possible, to try and turn any trenches which were met with. Within the terms of this instruction lies the root of our failure to make use of the priceless daylight hours of the 8th of August.

Normally, it may be correct to say that in modern

warfare infantry cannot be expected to advance without artillery preparation. But in a landing on a hostile shore the order has to be inverted. The infantry must advance and seize a suitable position to cover the landing, and to provide artillery positions for the main thrust. The very existence of the force, its water supply, its facilities for munitions and supplies, its power to reinforce, must absolutely depend on the infantry being able instantly to make good sufficient ground without the aid of the artillery other than can be supplied for the purpose by *floating* batteries.

" INERTIA "

This is not a condition that should take the commander of a covering force by surprise. It is one already foreseen. Driving power was required, and even a certain ruthlessness, to brush aside pleas for a respite for tired troops. The one fatal error was inertia. And inertia prevailed.

Late in the evening of the 7th the enemy had withdrawn the few guns which had been in action during the day. Beyond half a dozen shells dropped from very long range into the bay in the early morning of the 8th, no enemy artillery fired that day in the Suvla area. The guns had evidently been moved back, lest they should be captured when we pushed forward. As for the entrenched positions, these, in the

ordinary acceptance of the term, were non-
existent.

The General Staff Officer whom I had sent on
to Suvla early in the morning of the 8th reported
by telegraph the absence of hostile gun-fire, the
small amount of rifle fire, and the enemy's apparent
weakness. He also drew attention to the inaction
of our own troops, and to the fact that golden
opportunities were being missed.

"ALL WAS NOT WELL AT SUVLA"

Before this message arrived at General Headquarters I had made up my mind, from the Corps
Commander's own reports, that all was not well
at Suvla. There was risk in cutting myself adrift,
even temporarily, from touch with the operations
at Anzac and Helles; but I did my best to provide
against any sudden call by leaving Major-General
W. P. Braithwaite, my Chief of the General Staff,
in charge, with instructions to keep me closely informed of events at the other two fronts; and,
having done this, I took ship and set out for Suvla.

On arrival at about 5 p.m. I boarded H.M.S.
Jonquil, where I found Corps Headquarters, and
where General Stopford informed me that the
General Officer commanding 11th Division was
confident of success in an attack he was to make at
dawn next morning (the 9th). I felt no such confidence. Beyond a small advance by a part of the
11th Division between the Chocolate Hills and
Ismail Oglu Tepe, and some further progress along

the Kiretch Tepe Sirt ridge by the 10th Division, the day of the 8th had been lost.

"A Priceless Twelve Hours" Lost!

The Commander of the 11th Division had, it seems, ordered strong patrols to be pushed forward so as to make good all the strong positions in advance which could be occupied without serious fighting; but, as he afterwards reported, "little was done in this respect." Thus a priceless twelve hours had already gone to help the chances of the Turkish reinforcements which were, I knew, both from naval and aerial sources, actually on the march for Suvla. But when I urged that even now, at the eleventh hour, the 11th Division should make a concerted attack upon the hills, I was met by a *non possumus.* The objections of the morning were no longer valid; the men were now well rested, watered, and fed. But the Divisional Commanders disliked the idea of an advance by night, and General Stopford did not care, it seemed, to force their hands.

So it came about that I was driven to see whether I could not, myself, put concentration of effort and purpose into the direction of the large number of men ashore. The Corps Commander made no objection. He declared himself to be as eager as I could be to advance. The representations made by the Divisional Commanders had seemed to him insuperable. If I could see my way to get

G

over them no one would be more pleased than himself.

"The Sands Running Out"

Accompanied by Commodore Roger Keyes and Lieutenant-Colonel Aspinall, of the Headquarters General Staff, I landed on the beach, where all seemed quiet and peaceful, and saw the Commander of the 11th Division, Major-General Hammersley. I warned him the sands were running out fast, and that by dawn the high ground to his front might very likely be occupied in force by the enemy. He saw the danger, but declared that it was a physical impossibility, at so late an hour (6 p.m.), to get out orders for a night attack, the troops being very much scattered. There was no other difficulty now, but this was insuperable; he could not recast his orders or get them round to his troops in time. But one brigade, the 32nd, was, so General Hammersley admitted, more or less concentrated and ready to move.

The General Staff Officer of the division, Colonel Neil Malcolm, a soldier of experience, on whose opinion I set much value, was consulted. He agreed that the 32nd Brigade was now in a position to act. I, therefore, issued a direct order that, even if it were only with this 32nd Brigade, the advance should begin at the earliest possible moment, so that a portion at least of the 11th Division should anticipate the Turkish reinforcements on the heights and dig themselves in there upon some good tactical point.

In taking upon myself the serious responsibility of thus dealing with a detail of divisional tactics I was careful to limit the scope of the interference. Beyond directing that the one brigade which was reported ready to move at once should try and make good the heights before the enemy got on to them I did nothing, and said not a word, calculated to modify or in any way affect the attack already planned for the morning. Out of the thirteen battalions which were to have advanced against the heights at dawn four were now to anticipate that movement by trying to make good the key of the enemy's position at once and under cover of darkness.

THE 32ND BRIGADE

I have not been able to get a clear and coherent account of the doings of the 32nd Brigade; but I have established the fact that it did not actually commence its advance till 4 a.m. on the 9th of August. The reason given is that the units of the brigade were scattered. In General Stopford's despatch he says that "one company of the 6th East Yorks Pioneer Battalion succeeded in getting to the top of the hill north of Anafarta Sagir, but the rest of the battalion and the 32nd Brigade were attacked from both flanks during their advance, and fell back to a line north and south of Sulajik.

Very few of the leading company or the Royal Engineers who accompanied it got back, and that evening the strength of the battalion was nine officers and 380 men."

After their retirement from the hill, north of Anafarta Sagir (which commanded the whole battlefield) this 32nd Brigade then still marked the high-water level of the advance made at dawn by the rest of the division. When their first retirement was completed they had to fall back further, so as to come into line with the most forward of their comrades. The inference seems clear. Just as the 32nd Brigade in their advance met with markedly less opposition than the troops who attacked an hour and a half later, so, had they themselves started earlier, they would probably have experienced less opposition. Further, it seems reasonable to suppose that, had the complete division started at 4 a.m. on the 9th, or, better still, at 10 p.m. on the 8th, they would have made good the whole of the heights in front of them.

That night I stayed at Suvla, preferring to drop direct cable contact with my operations as a whole to losing touch with a corps battle which seemed to be going wrong.

A Bad Moment

At dawn on the 9th I watched General Hammersley's attack, and very soon realised by the

well-sustained artillery fire of the enemy (so silent
the previous day), and by the volume of the
musketry, that Turkish reinforcements had arrived;
that with the renewed confidence caused by our
long delay the guns had been brought back; and
that, after all, we were forestalled. This was a
bad moment. Our attack failed; our losses were
very serious. The enemy's enfilading shrapnel
fire seemed to be especially destructive and de-
moralising, the shell bursting low and all along
our line. Time after time it threw back our
attack just as it seemed upon the point of making
good.

The 33rd Brigade at first made most hopeful
progress in its attempt to seize Ismail Oglu Tepe.
Some of the leading troops gained the summit, and
were able to look over on to the other side. Many
Turks were killed here. Then the centre seemed
to give way. Whether this was the result of the
shrapnel fire or whether, as some say, an order
to retire came up from the rear, the result was
equally fatal to success. As the centre fell back
the steady, gallant behaviour of the 6th Battalion
Border Regiment, and the 6th Battalion Lincoln
Regiment, on either flank was especially note-
worthy. Scrub fires on Hill 70 did much to harass
and hamper our troops.

When the 32nd Brigade fell back before attacks
from the slopes of the hill north of Anafarta Sagir
and from the direction of Abrijka they took up
the line north and south through Sulajik. Here
their left was protected by two battalions of the

34th Brigade, which came up to their support. The line was later on prolonged by the remainder of the 34th Brigade and two battalions of the 159th Brigade of the 53rd Division. Their right was connected with the Chocolate Hills by the 33rd Brigade on the position to which they had returned after their repulse from the upper slopes of Ismail Oglu Tepe.

THE GALLANT HEREFORDS

Some of the units which took part in this engagement acquitted themselves very bravely. I regret I have not had sufficient detail given me to enable me to mention them by name. The Divisional Commander speaks with appreciation of one freshly landed battalion of the 53rd Division, a Hereford battalion, presumably the 1/1st Herefordshire, which attacked with impetuosity and courage between Hetman Chair and Kaslar Chair, about Azmak Dere, on the extreme right of his line.

During the night of the 8th/9th and early morning of the 9th the whole of the 53rd (Territorial) Division (my general reserve) had arrived and disembarked. I had ordered it up to Suvla, hoping that by adding its strength to the 9th Corps General Stopford might still be enabled to secure the commanding ground round the bay. The infantry brigades of the 53rd Division (no artillery had accompanied it from England) reinforced the 11th Division.

ANAFARTA RIDGE AGAIN

On August 10th the Corps Commander decided to make another attempt to take the Anafarta ridge. The 11th Division were not sufficiently rested to play a prominent part in the operation, but the 53rd Division, under General Lindley, was to attack, supported by General Hammersley. On the 10th there were one brigade of Royal Field Artillery ashore, with two mountain batteries, and all the ships' guns were available to co-operate. But the attack failed, though the Corps Commander considers that seasoned troops would have succeeded, especially as the enemy were showing signs of being shaken by our artillery fire. General Stopford points out, however, and rightly so, that the attack was delivered over very difficult country, and that it was a high trial for troops who had never been in action before, and with no regulars to set a standard.

ENEMY ABLY COMMANDED

Many of the battalions fought with great gallantry, and were led forward with much devotion by their officers. At a moment when things were looking dangerous two battalions of the 11th Division (not specified by the Corps Commander) rendered very good service on the left of the Territorials. At the end of the day our troops occupied the line Hill east of Chocolate Hills— Sulajik, whilst the enemy—who had been ably commanded throughout—were still receiving reinforcements, and, apart from their artillery, were three times as strong as they had been on the 7th August.

Orders were issued to the General Officer Commanding 9th Corps to take up and entrench a line across the whole front from near the Azmak Dere, through the knoll east of the Chocolate Hills, to the ground held by the 10th Division about Kiretch Tepe Sirt. General Stopford took advantage of this opportunity to reorganise the divisions, and, as there was a gap in the line between the left of the 53rd Division and the right of the 10th Division, gave orders for the preparation of certain strong points to enable it to be held.

The 54th Division (infantry only) arrived, and were disembarked on August 11th and placed in reserve. On the following day—August 12th—I proposed that the 54th Division should make a night march in order to attack, at dawn on the 13th, the heights Kavak Tepe—Teke Tepe. The Corps Commander, having reason to believe that the enclosed country about Kuchuk Anafarta Ova and to the north of it was held by the enemy, ordered one brigade to move forward in advance, and make good Kuchuk Anafarta Ova, so as to ensure an unopposed march for the remainder of the division as far as that place. So that afternoon the 163rd Brigade moved off, and, in spite of serious opposition, established itself about the A. of Anafarta (118 m. 4 and 7), in difficult and enclosed country.

THE ARDENT NORFOLKS

In the course of the fight, creditable in all respects to the 163rd Brigade, there happened a very mysterious thing. The 1/5th Norfolks were on the right of the line, and found themselves for a moment less strongly opposed than the rest of the brigade. Against the yielding forces of the enemy Colonel Sir H. Beauchamp, a bold, self-confident officer, eagerly pressed forward, followed by the best part of the battalion. The fighting grew hotter, and the ground became more wooded and broken. At this stage many men were wounded or grew exhausted with thirst. These found their way back to camp during the night. But the Colonel, with sixteen officers and 250 men, still kept pushing on, driving the enemy before him. Amongst these ardent souls was part of a fine company enlisted from the King's Sandringham estates. Nothing more was ever seen or heard of any of them. They charged into the forest, and were lost to sight or sound. Not one of them ever came back.

PROJECTED ATTACK ABANDONED

The night march and projected attack were now abandoned, owing to the Corps Commander's representations as to the difficulties of keeping the division supplied with food, water, etc., even should they gain the height. General Birdwood had hoped he would soon be able to make a fresh attack on Sari Bair, provided that he might reckon on a corresponding vigorous advance to be made by the 11th and 54th Divisions on Ismail Oglu Tepe. On August 13th I so informed General Stopford. But when it came to business, General Birdwood found he could not yet carry out his new attack on Sari Bair—and, indeed, could only help the 9th Corps with one brigade from Damak-jelik Bair. I was obliged, therefore, to abandon this project for the nonce, and directed General Stopford to confine his attention to strengthening his line across his present front. To straighten out the left of this line General Stopford ordered the General Officer Commanding the 10th Division to advance on the following day (15th August), so as to gain possession of the crest of the Kiretch Tepe Sirt, the 54th Division to co-operate.

The 30th and 31st Infantry Brigades of the 10th Irish Division were to attack frontally along the high ridge. The 162nd Infantry Brigade of the 54th Division were to support on the right. The infantry were to be seconded by a machine-gun detachment of the Royal Naval Air Service, by the guns of H.M.S. *Grampus* and H.M.S. *Foxhound* from the Gulf of Saros, by the Argyll Mountain Battery, the 15th Heavy Battery, and the 58th Field Battery. After several hours of indecisive artillery and musketry fighting, the 6th

Royal Dublin Fusiliers charged forward with loud cheers, and captured the whole ridge, together with eighteen prisoners.

NAVAL GUNS SUPPORT

The vigorous support rendered by the naval guns was a feature of this operation. Unfortunately, the point of the ridge was hard to hold, and means for maintaining the forward trenches had not been well thought out. Casualties became very heavy, the 5th Royal Irish Fusiliers having only one officer left, and the 5th Inniskilling Fusiliers also losing heavily in officers. Reinforcements were promised, but before they could arrive the officer left in command decided to evacuate the front trenches. The strength of the Turks opposed to us was steadily rising, and had now reached 20,000.

GENERAL STOPFORD HANDS OVER COMMAND TO MAJOR-GENERAL DE LISLE

On the evening of the 15th August General Stopford handed over command of the 9th Corps.

The units of the 10th and 11th Divisions had shown their mettle when they leaped into the water to get more quickly to close quarters, or when they stormed Lala Baba in the darkness.

They had shown their resolution later when they tackled the Chocolate Hills and drove the enemy from Hill 10 right back out of rifle range from the beaches.

Then had come hesitation. The advantage had not been pressed. The senior Commanders at Suvla had had no personal experience of the new trench warfare; of the Turkish methods; of the paramount importance of time. Strong, clear leadership had not been promptly enough applied. These were the reasons which induced me, with your Lordship's approval, to appoint Major-General H. de B. De Lisle to take over temporary command.

ORGANISING FRESH ATTACKS

I had already seen General De Lisle on his way from Cape Helles, and my formal instructions— full copy in Appendix—were handed to him by my Chief of the General Staff. Under these he was to make it his most pressing business to get the Corps into fighting trim again, so that as big a proportion of it as possible might be told off for a fresh attack upon Ismail Oglu Tepe and the Anafarta spur. At his disposal were placed the 10th Division (less one brigade), the 11th Division, the 53rd and 54th Divisions—a force imposing enough on paper, but totalling, owing to casualties, under 30,000 rifles.

The fighting strength of ourselves and of our

adversaries stood at this time at about the following figures :—Lieutenant-General Birdwood commanded 25,000 rifles, at Anzac; Lieutenant-General Davies, in the southern zone, commanded 23,000 rifles; whilst the French corps alongside of him consisted of some 17,000 rifles. The Turks had been very active in the south, doubtless to prevent us reinforcing Anzac or Suvla; but it is doubtful if there were more than 35,000 of them in that region. The bulk of the enemy were engaged against Anzac or were in reserve in the valleys east and north of Sari Bair. Their strength was estimated at 75,000 rifles.

Enemy's Advantages

The Turks then, I reckoned, had 110,000 rifles to our 95,000, and held all the vantages of ground; they had plenty of ammunition, also drafts wherewith to refill ranks depleted in action within two or three days. My hopes that these drafts would be of poor quality had been every time disappointed. After weighing all these points, I sent your Lordship a long cable. In it I urged that if the campaign was to be brought to a quick, victorious decision, large reinforcements must at once be sent out. Autumn, I pointed out, was already upon us, and there was not a moment to be lost. At that time (16th August) my British divisions alone were 45,000 under establishment, and some of my fine battalions had dwindled down so far that I had to withdraw them from the fighting line. Our most vital need was the replenishment of these sadly depleted ranks. When that was done I wanted 50,000 fresh rifles. From what I knew of the Turkish situation, both in its local and general aspects, it seemed, humanly speaking, a certainty that if this help could be sent to me *at once* we could still clear a passage for our fleet to Constantinople.

No Reinforcements

It may be judged, then, how deep was my disappointment when I learnt that the essential drafts, reinforcements, and munitions could not be sent to me, the reason given being one which prevented me from any further insistence. So I resolved to do my very best with the means at my disposal, and forthwith reinforced the northern wing with the 2nd Mounted Division (organised as dismounted troops) from Egypt and the 29th Division from the southern area. These movements and the work of getting the 9th Corps and attached divisions into battle array took time, and it was not until the 21st that I was ready to renew the attack—an attack to be carried out under very different conditions from those of the 7th and 8th August.

The enemy's positions were now being rapidly entrenched, and, as I could not depend on receiving reinforcing drafts, I was faced with the danger that if I could not drive the Turks back I might lose so many men that I would find myself unable to hold the very extensive new area of ground which had been gained. I therefore decided to mass every available man against Ismail Oglu Tepe, a *sine quâ non* to my plans whether as a first step towards clearing the valley, or, if this proved impossible, towards securing Suvla Bay and Anzac Cove from shell fire.

A Well-planned Attack

The scheme for this attack was well planned by General De Lisle. The 53rd and 54th Divisions were to hold the enemy from Sulajik to Kiretch Tepe Sirt while the 29th Division and 11th Division stormed Ismail Oglu Tepe. Two brigades, 10th Division, and the 2nd Mounted Division were retained in Corps Reserve. I arranged that General Birdwood should co-operate by swinging forward his left flank to Susuk Kuyu and Kaiajik Aghala. Naturally I should have liked still further to extend the scope of my attack by ordering an advance of the 9th Corps all along their line, but many of the battalions had been too highly tried, and I felt it was unwise to call upon them for another effort so soon. The attack would only be partial, but it was an essential attack if any real progress was to be made. Also, once the Anafarta ridge was in my hands the enemy would be unable to reinforce through the gap between the two Anafartas, and then, so I believed, my left would find no difficulty in getting on.

GOAT TRACKS BETWEEN BUSHES

My special objective was the hill which forms the south-west corner of the Anafarta Sagir spur. Ismail Oglu Tepe, as it is called, forms a strong natural barrier against an invader from the Ægean who might wish to march direct against the Anafartas. The hill rises 350 feet from the plain, with steep spurs jutting out to the west and south-west, the whole of it covered with dense holly oak scrub, so nearly impenetrable that it breaks up an attack and forces troops to move in single file along goat tracks between the bushes. The comparatively small number of guns landed up to date was a weakness, seeing we had now to storm trenches, but the battleships were there to back us, and as the bombardment was limited to a narrow front of a mile it was hoped the troops would find themselves able to carry the trenches and that the impetus of the charge would carry them up to the top of the crest.

Our chief difficulty lay in the open nature and shallow depth of the ground available for the concentration for attack. The only cover we possessed was the hill Lala Baba, 200 yards from the sea, and Yilghin Burnu, half a mile from the Turkish front, the ground between these two being an exposed plain. The 29th Division, which was to make the attack on the left, occupied the front trenches during the preceding night; the 11th Division, which

MAP 5.

was to attack on the right, occupied the front trenches on the right of Yilghin Burnu.

H

MIST PROTECTS TURKS

By some freak of nature Suvla Bay and plain were wrapped in a strange mist on the afternoon of the 21st of August. This was sheer bad luck, as we had reckoned on the enemy's gunners being blinded by the declining sun and upon the Turkish trenches being shown up by the evening light with singular clearness, as would have been the case on ninety-nine days out of a hundred. Actually we could hardly see the enemy lines this afternoon, whereas out to the westward targets stood out in strong relief against the luminous mist. I wished to postpone the attack, but for various reasons this was not possible and so from 2.30 p.m. to 3 p.m. a heavy but none too accurate artillery bombardment from land and sea was directed against the Turkish first line of trenches, whilst twenty-four machine-guns in position on Yilghin Burnu did what they could to lend a hand.

"NORTH-EAST INSTEAD OF EAST"

At 3 p.m. an advance was begun by the infantry on the right of the line. The 34th Brigade of the 11th Division rushed the Turkish trenches between Hetman Chair and Aire Kavak, practically without loss, but the 32nd Brigade, directed against Hetman Chair and the communication trench connecting that point with the south-west corner of the Ismail Oglu Tepe spur, failed to make good its point. The brigade had lost direction in the first instance, moving north-east instead of east, and though it attempted to carry the communication trench from the north-east with great bravery and great disregard of life, it never succeeded in rectifying the original mistake. The 33rd Brigade, sent up in haste with orders to capture this communication trench at all costs, fell into precisely the same error, part of it marching north-east and part south-east to Susuk Kuyu.

Meanwhile the 29th Division, whose attack had been planned for 3.30 p.m., had attacked Scimitar Hill (Hill 70) with great dash. The 87th Brigade, on the left, carried the trenches on Scimitar Hill, but the 86th Brigade were checked and upset by a raging forest fire across their front. Eventually pressing on, they found themselves unable to advance up the valley between the two spurs owing to the failure of the 32nd Brigade of the 11th Division on their right.

The brigade then tried to attack eastwards, but were decimated by a cross-fire of shell and musketry from the north and south-east. The leading troops were simply swept off the top of the spur, and had to fall back to a ledge south-west of Scimitar Hill, where they found a little cover. Whilst this fighting was in progress the 2nd Mounted Division moved out from Lala Baba in open formation to take up a position of readiness behind Yilghin Burnu. During this march they came under a remarkably steady and accurate artillery fire.

THE YEOMEN OF ENGLAND

The advance of these English Yeomen was a sight calculated to send a thrill of pride through anyone with a drop of English blood running in their veins. Such superb martial spectacles are rare in modern war. Ordinarily it should always be possible to bring up reserves under some sort of cover from shrapnel fire. Here, for a mile and a half, there was nothing to conceal a mouse, much less some of the most stalwart soldiers England has ever sent from her shores. Despite the critical events in other parts of the field, I could hardly take my glasses from the Yeomen; they moved like men marching on parade. Here and there a shell would take toll of a cluster; there they lay; there was no straggling; the others moved steadily on; not a man was there who hung back or hurried. But such an ordeal must consume some of the battle-winning fighting energy of those subjected to it, and it is lucky indeed for the Turks that the terrain, as well as the lack of trenches, forbade us from letting the 2nd Mounted Division loose at close quarters to the enemy without undergoing this previous too heavy baptism of fire.

BUSH FIRES AND MUSKETRY

Now that the 11th Division had made their effort, and failed, the 2nd South Midland Brigade (commanded by Brigadier-General Earl of Longford) was sent forward from its position of readiness behind Yilghin Burnu, in the hope that they might yet restore the fortunes of the day. This brigade, in action for the first time, encountered both bush fires and musketry without flinching, but the advance had in places to be almost by inches, and the actual close attack by the Yeomen did not take place until night was fast falling. On the left they reached the foremost line of the 29th Division, and on the right also they got as far as the leading battalions. But, as soon as it was dark, one regiment pushed up the valley between Scimitar Hill and Hill 100 (on Ismail Oglu Tepe), and carried the trenches on a small knoll near the centre of this horseshoe.

The regiment imagined it had captured Hill 100, which would have been a very notable success, enabling as it would the whole of our line to hang on and dig in. But when the report came in some doubt was felt as to its accuracy, and a reconnaissance by staff officers showed that the knoll was a good way from Hill 100, and that a strongly held semi-circle of Turkish trenches (the enemy having been heavily reinforced) still denied us access to the top of the hill. As the men were too done, and had lost too heavily to admit of a second immediate assault, and as the knoll actually held would have been swept by fire at daybreak, there was nothing for it but to fall back under cover of darkness to our original line. The losses in this attack fell most heavily on the 29th Division. They were just under 5,000.

THE 2ND SOUTH MIDLAND BRIGADE

I am sorry not to be able to give more detail as to the conduct of individuals and units during this battle. But the 2nd South Midland Brigade has been brought to my notice, and it consisted of the Bucks Yeomanry, the Berks Yeomanry, and the Dorset Yeomanry. The Yeomanry fought very bravely, and on personal, as well as public, grounds I specially deplore the loss of Brigadier-General Earl of Longford, K.P., M.V.O., and Brigadier-General P. A. Kenna, V.C., D.S.O., A.D.C.

The same day, as pre-arranged with General Birdwood, a force consisting of two battalions of New Zealand Mounted Rifles, two battalions of the 29th Irish Brigade, the 4th South Wales Borderers, and 29th Indian Infantry Brigade, the whole under the command of Major-General H. V. Cox, was working independently to support the main attack.

General Cox divided his force into three sections : the left section to press forward and establish a permanent hold on the existing lightly held outpost line covering the junction of the 11th Division with the Anzac front; the centre section to seize the well at Kabak Kuyu, an asset of utmost value, whether to ourselves or the enemy; the right section to attack and capture the Turkish trenches on the north-east side of the Kaiajik Aghala.

INDIANS SEIZE A WELL

The advance of the left section was a success; after a brisk engagement the well at Kabak Kuyu was seized by the Indian Brigade, and, by 4.30, the right column, under Brigadier-General Russell, under heavy fire, effected a lodgment on the Kaiajik Aghala, where our men entrenched, and began to dig communications across the Kaiajik Dere towards the lines of the 4th Australian Brigade south of the Dere. A pretty stiff bomb fight ensued, in which General Russell's troops held their own through the night against superior force.

At 6 a.m. on the morning of the 22nd August General Russell, reinforced by the newly arrived 18th Australian Battalion, attacked the summit of the Kaiajik Aghala. The Australians carried 150 yards of the trenches, losing heavily in so doing, and were then forced to fall back again owing to enfilade fire, though in the meantime the New Zealand Mounted Rifles managed, in spite of constant counter-attacks, to make good another 80 yards.

A counter-attack in strength launched by the Turks at 10 a.m. was repulsed; the new line from the Kaiajik Aghala to Susuk Kuyu was gradually strengthened, and eventually joined on to the right of the 9th Army Corps, thereby materially improving the whole situation. During this action the 4th Australian Brigade, which remained facing the Turks on the upper part of the Kaiajik Aghala, was able to inflict several hundred casualties on the enemy as they retreated or endeavoured to reinforce.

REPULSED, BUT NOT DEFEATED

On the 21st of August we had carried the Turkish entrenchments at several points, but had been unable to hold what we had gained except along the section where Major-General Cox had made a good advance with Anzac and Indian troops. To be repulsed is not to be defeated, as long as the commander and his troops are game to renew the attack.

All were eager for such a renewal of the offensive; but clearly we would have for some time to possess our souls in patience, seeing that reinforcements and munitions were short, that we were already outnumbered by the enemy, and that a serious outbreak of sickness showed how it had become imperative to give a spell of rest to the men who had been fighting so magnificently and so continuously.

To calculate on rest, it may be suggested, was to calculate without the enemy. Such an idea has no true bearing on the feelings of the garrison of the peninsula. That the Turks should attack had always been the earnest prayer of all of us, just as much after the 21st August as before it. And now that we had to suspend progress for a bit, work was put in hand upon the line from Suvla to Anzac, a minor offensive routine of sniping and bombing was organised, and, in a word, trench warfare set in on both sides.

LIEUTENANT-GENERAL BYNG ASSUMES COMMAND

On 24th August Lieutenant-General the Hon. J. H. G. Byng, K.C.M.G., C.B., M.V.O., assumed command of the 9th Army Corps.

The last days of the month were illumined by a brilliant affair carried through by the troops under General Birdwood's command. Our object was to complete the capture of Hill 60 north of the Kaiajik Aghala, commenced by Major-General Cox on the 21st August. Hill 60 overlooked the Biyuk Ana-farta valley, and was therefore tactically a very important feature.

HOT FIRE FROM THE ENEMY

The conduct of the attack was again entrusted to Major-General Cox, at whose disposal were placed detachments from the 4th and 5th Australian Brigades, the New Zealand Mounted Rifles Brigade, and the 5th Connaught Rangers. The advance was timed to take place at 5 p.m. on the 27th of August, after the heaviest artillery bombardment we could afford.

This bombardment seemed effective; but the moment the assailants broke cover they were greeted by an exceeding hot fire from the enemy field-guns, rifles, and machine-guns, followed after a brief interval by a shower of heavy shell, some of which, most happily, pitched into the trenches of the Turks. On the right the detachment from the 4th and 5th Australian Brigades could make no headway against a battery of machine-guns which confronted them. In the centre the New Zealanders made a most determined onslaught, and carried one side of the topmost knoll. Hand-to-hand fighting continued here till 9.30 p.m., when it was reported that nine-tenths of the summit had been gained.

On the left the 250 men of the 5th Connaught Rangers excited the admiration of all beholders by the swiftness and cohesion of their charge. In five minutes they had carried their objective, the northern Turkish communications, when they at once set to and began a lively bomb-fight along the trenches against strong parties which came hurrying up from the enemy supports and afterwards from their reserves. At midnight fresh troops were to have strengthened our grip upon the hill, but before that hour the Irishmen had been out-bombed, and the 9th Australian Light Horse, who had made a most plucky attempt to recapture the lost communication trench, had been repulsed. Luckily, the New Zealand Mounted Rifles refused to recognise that they were worsted. Nothing would shift them. All that night and all next day, through bombing, bayonet charges, musketry, shrapnel, and heavy shell, they hung on to their 150 yards of trench. At 1 a.m. on August 29th

the 10th Light Horse made another attack on the
lost communication trenches to the left, carried
them, and finally held them.   This gave us complete command of the under-feature, an outlook
over the Anafarta Sagir valley, and safer lateral
communications between Anzac and Suvla Bay.

TURKS LOSE 5,000

Our casualties in this hotly contested affair
amounted to 1,000.   The Turks lost out of all proportion more.   Their line of retreat was commanded from our Kaiajik Dere trenches, whence
our observers were able to direct artillery fire
equally upon their fugitives and their reinforcements.   The same observers estimated the Turkish
casualties as no less than 5,000.   Three Turkish
machine-guns and forty-six prisoners were taken,
as well as three trench mortars, 300 Turkish rifles,
60,000 rounds of ammunition, and 500 bombs.
Four hundred acres were added to the territories
of Anzac.   Major-General Cox showed his usual
forethought and wisdom.   Brigadier-General Russell
fought his men splendidly.

CONFIDENT AND CHEERFUL TROOPS

My narrative of battle incidents must end here.
From this date onwards up to the date of my

departure on October 17th the flow of munitions and drafts fell away. Sickness, the legacy of a desperately trying summer, took heavy toll of the survivors of so many arduous conflicts. No longer was there any question of operations on the grand scale, but with such troops it was difficult to be downhearted. All ranks were cheerful; all remained confident that, so long as they stuck to their guns, their country would stick to them, and see them victoriously through the last and greatest of the crusades.

Evacuation "Unthinkable"

On the 11th October your Lordship cabled asking me for an estimate of the losses which would be involved in an evacuation of the peninsula. On the 12th October I replied in terms showing that such a step was to me unthinkable. On the 16th October I received a cable recalling me to London for the reason, as I was informed by your Lordship on my arrival, that His Majesty's Government desired a fresh, unbiassed opinion, from a responsible Commander, upon the question of early evacuation.

In bringing this despatch to a close I wish to refer gratefully to the services rendered by certain formations, whose work has so far only been recognised by a sprinkling of individual rewards.

ROYAL NAVAL AIR SERVICE

Much might be written on the exploits of the Royal Naval Air Service, but these bold flyers are laconic, and their feats will mostly pass unrecorded. Yet let me here thank them, with their Commander, Colonel F. H. Sykes, of the Royal Marines, for the nonchalance with which they appear to affront danger and death, when and where they can. So doing, they quicken the hearts of their friends on land and sea—an asset of greater military value even than their bombs or aerial reconnaissances, admirable in all respects as these were.

With them I also couple the *Service de l'Aviation* of the *Corps Expéditionnaire d'Orient,* who daily wing their way in and out of the shrapnel under the distinguished leadership of M. le Capitaine Césari.

The Armoured Car Division (Royal Naval Air Service) have never failed to respond to any call which might be made upon them. Their organisation was broken up; their work had to be carried out under strange conditions—from the bows of the *River Clyde,* as independent batteries attached to infantry divisions, etc., etc.—and yet they were always cheerful, always ready to lend a hand in any sort of fighting that might give them a chance of settling old scores with the enemy.

THE ROYAL ARTILLERY

Next I come to the Royal Artillery. By their constant vigilance, by their quick grasp of the key to every emergency, by their thundering good shooting, by hundreds of deeds of daring, they have earned the unstinted admiration of all their comrade services. Where all fought so remarkably the junior officers deserve a little niche of their own in the Dardanelles record of fame. Their audacity in reconnaissance, their insouciance under the hottest of fires, stand as a fine example not only to the Army, but to the nation at large.

Heroic Stretcher-bearers

A feature of every report, narrative, or diary I have read has been a tribute to the stretcher-bearers. All ranks, from Generals in command to wounded men in hospital, are unanimous in their praise. I have watched a party from the moment when the telephone summoned them from their dug-out to the time when they returned with their wounded. To see them run light-heartedly across fire-swept slopes is to be privileged to witness a superb example of the hero in man. No braver corps exists, and I believe the reason to be that all thought of self is instinctively flung aside when the saving of others is the motive.

Drafts, Munitions, and Supplies

The services rendered by Major-General (temporary Lieutenant-General) E. A. Altham, C.B.,

C.M.G., Inspector-General of Communications, and all the Departments and Services of the Lines of Communication assured us a life-giving flow of drafts, munitions, and supplies. The work was carried out under unprecedented conditions, and is deserving, I submit, of handsome recognition.

With General Altham were associated Brigadier-General (temporary Major-General) C. R. R. McGrigor, C.B., at first Commandant of the Base at Alexandria and later Deputy Inspector-General of Communications, and Colonel T. E. O'Leary, Deputy Adjutant-General, 3rd Echelon. Both of these officers carried out their difficult duties to my entire satisfaction.

My Military Secretary, Lieutenant-Colonel S. H. Pollen, has displayed first-class ability in the conduct of his delicate and responsible duties.

Also I take the opportunity of my last despatch to mention two of my Aides-de-Camp—Major F. L. Magkill-Crichton-Maitland, Gordon Highlanders, Lieutenant Hon. G. St. J. Brodrick, Surrey Yeomanry.

I have many other names to bring to notice for distinguished and gallant service during the operations under review, and these will form the subject of a separate communication.

TRIBUTE TO THE DEAD

And now, before affixing to this despatch my final signature as Commander-in-Chief of the

Mediterranean Expeditionary Force, let me first pay tribute to the everlasting memory of my dear comrades who will return no more. Next, let me thank each and all, Generals, Staff, Regimental Leaders, and rank and file, for their wonderful loyalty, patience, and self-sacrifice. Our progress was constant, and if it was painfully slow—they know the truth. So I bid them all farewell with a special God-speed to the campaigners who have served with me right through from the terrible yet most glorious earlier days—the incomparable 29th Division; the young veterans of the Naval Division; the ever-victorious Australians and New Zealanders; the stout East Lancs., and my own brave fellow-countrymen of the Lowland Division of Scotland.

I have the honour to be,

Your Lordship's most obedient servant,

IAN HAMILTON,

General, Commander-in-Chief,
Mediterranean Expeditionary Force.

PRINTED IN GREAT BRITAIN BY R. CLAY AND SONS, LTD.,
BRUNSWICK STREET, STAMFORD STREET, S.E., AND BUNGAY, SUFFOLK.

www.ingramcontent.com/pod-product-compliance
Lightning Source LLC
Chambersburg PA
CBHW030932150426
42812CB00064B/2799/J